PEOPLE STILL TALKIN

"Geezumpiece! This is the best
It's so professional and well pu

"This is long overdue! I love the
encapsulates all of our Cayman words. Unna really need ta
read dis book!" -- **Dara Flowers Burke**

"I think this is a brilliant mode of capturing, preserving and transcending our linguistic culture which is unique but constantly changing. As a pivotal document in the literary arts it can be utilised as an educational tool, tourist/cultural guide and a historical manuscript for us to reflect and reminisce of our yesteryears. Well done!" -- **Anthony Ramoon**

"As we grow up and educate our children, we should always remember what makes us uniquely Caymanian, and what better way than to have a reference within our reach. I love it!" -- **Tania Ebanks**

"This document brings forward a lot of our culture that has been overlooked for quite some time. My hope is that it will be used in the schools as a cultural tool for future generations." -- **Brainard D. Watler**

"At last! Great insight! Exactly what Cayman needed. This will cement and further showcase a very important piece of our unique culture locally and worldwide. What better way than through our local dialect?" -- **Merta Day**

"This is the perfect book to help us understand dem older Caymanians when they get to telling their old time stories. It's an absolutely essential educational tool for the younger generation to learn their linguistic history." -- **Devon Edie**

"I am excited about the Cayman Islands Dictionary! Now my children can look up all the 'crazy' words and expressions that I use and I might actually start to make some sense to them! -- **Delores Thompson**

"This is definitely a wake-up call for those who take our heritage for granted. Hopefully it will inspire our people to delve into things Caymanian instead of recycling other cultures." -- **Cara Anderson**

"In today's society it seems like each of our generations are losing pieces of our culture. This dictionary is an invaluable tool that preserves our culture and proves to be a real eye opener." -- **David Goddard**

"At Last! Cayman has its own first illustration of spoken word, culture and identity, in the Cayman Islands Dictionary. A must read for Caymanians, as well as anyone who wants to be 'in the know' about being a Caymanian." -- **Kim Wallace-Watler**

"It's amazing that someone would think about writing a dictionary just for Cayman! What a great legacy to leave for our children." -- **Victor Thompson**

"A Caymanian Dictionary? Why didn't I think of that?"
-- **Morris Martin**

"Spoken word is an integral component of any culture. To that end, this Dictionary takes a stab at truly defining that component which is Caymanian culture!" -- **Daniel Reid**

"This dictionary should be taught in all of the schools, both private and public. Our children need to learn more about our heritage so that they may pass it on to their children."
-- **Marcia Finnikin (Watler)**

"Awlehkipitins! It's about time we had our own dictionary. This is the perfect marriage between Cayman's traditional past and its contemporary future." -- **Maxwell Linwood**

"Finally, a way for the older people to understand the current generation. Now they don't have to ask "wah dis mean?" and "wah dat mean?" -- **Carla Martin**

WWW.CAYMANISLANDS.KY

Welcome to the Cayman Islands

HE HATH FOUNDED IT UPON THE SEAS

Our Discovery Day
The explorer Christopher Columbus discovered the Cayman Islands on 10 May 1503.

The Cayman Islands

The Cayman Islands is a British Overseas Territory located in the Caribbean Sea. The Islands are comprised of Grand Cayman (the capital), Cayman Brac and Little Cayman and are world reknown as a major offshore financial centre and coveted tourist destination.

BRIEF HISTORY

Christopher Columbus (left) first sighted Cayman Brac and Little Cayman on 10 May 1503. On his fourth trip to the New World, Columbus was en route to Hispaniola when his ship was thrust westward toward *"two very small and low islands, full of tortoises, as was all the sea all about, insomuch that they looked like little rocks, for which reason these islands were called Las Tortugas."*

A 1523 map shows all three Islands with the name *Lagartos*, meaning 'alligators' or 'large lizards', but by 1530 the name '*Caymanas*' was being used. It is derived from the Carib Indian word for the marine crocodile ('*caiman*'), which is now known to have lived in the Islands.

Sir Francis Drake, on his 1585-86 voyage, reported seeing *"great serpents called Caymanas, like large lizards, which are edible."*

It was the Islands' ample supply of turtle, however, that made them a popular calling place for ships sailing the Caribbean and in need of meat for their crews.

"For He hath founded it upon the seas and established it upon the waters."

-- Psalm 24: 2

This began a trend that eventually denuded local waters of the turtle, compelling local turtle fishermen to go further afield to Cuba and the Miskito Cays in search of their catch.

The first recorded settlements were located on Little Cayman and Cayman Brac during 1661-71. Because of the depredations of Spanish privateers, the Governor of Jamaica called the settlers back to Jamaica, though by this time Spain had recognised British possession of the Islands in the 1670 Treaty of Madrid. Often in breach of the treaty, British privateers roamed the area taking their prizes, probably using the Cayman Islands to replenish stocks of food and water and careen their vessels.

Though Cayman was regarded as a dependency of Jamaica, the reins of government by that colony were loosely held in the early years, and a tradition grew of self-government, with matters of public concern decided at meetings of all free males. In 1831 a legislative assembly was established.

The constitutional relationship between Cayman and Jamaica remained ambiguous until 1863 when an act of the British parliament formally made the Cayman Islands a dependency of Jamaica. When Jamaica achieved independence in 1962, the Islands opted to remain under the British Crown, and an administrator appointed from London assumed the responsibilities previously held by the governor of Jamaica

The constitution currently provides for a Crown-appointed Governor, a Legislative Assembly and a Cabinet. Unless there are exceptional reasons, the Governor accepts the advice of the Cabinet, which comprises three appointed official members and five ministers elected from the 15 elected members of the Assembly. The Governor has responsibility for the police, civil service, defence and external affairs but handed over the presidency of the Legislative Assembly to the Speaker in 1991.

Source: www.gov.ky

BASIC CHRONOLOGY

1503: Discovered by Christopher Columbus.

Named *"Las Tortugas"* (The Turtles) after the numerous sea turtles.

1586: First recorded English visitor, Sir Francis Drake re-names the islands *"Cayman Islands"* after the Spanish term *'Caiman'* which means crocodile.

1587-1699: Islands remained uninhabited.

1670: The Islands, along with neighbouring Jamaica were captured then ceded to England under the Treaty of Madrid.

1700: Isaac Bodden (born on Grand Cayman), became the first recorded permanent inhabitant of the Cayman Islands. It is said that he was the grandson of the original settler named *Boden* who arrived in Cayman via Jamaica in 1655.

1962: Jamaica wins independence from England. Cayman Islands become a separate British Overseas Territory.

1972: First ever Constitution allows election of a local government, granting greater autonomy to pursue its own goals.

2003: Quincentennial Celebrations mark 500 years of growth and prosperity.

Sources: www.gov.ky and Cayman Islands National Archive

BASIC FACTS

Capital: George Town, Grand Cayman.

Demonym: Caymanian

Government: British Overseas Territory

- **Monarch:** HM Queen Elizabeth II
- **Governor:** HE Martyn Roper, OBE
- **Premier:** Hon. Alden McLaughlin, JP, MBE

Legislature: Legislative Assembly

Establishment: British Overseas Territory (1962)
Current Constitution (Nov. 2010)

Area: Total: 264 km² (206th) / 102 mi²
Water %: 1.6

Population: 64,420, as of Spring 2018
Density: 212/km2 (57th)
549/sq mi

GDP: 2017 Estimate:
- **Real GDP:** $2,786.8 (CI$M)
- **Per Capita:** $44,154

Currency: Cayman Islands Dollar (KYD)

Internet TLD: .ky

Calling Code: +1.345

Time Zone: - UTC-5)
- Summer (DST)

Sources: www.gov.ky and www.eso.ky

The Cayman Islands

A British Overseas Territory located approximately 480 miles southeast of Miami, Florida.

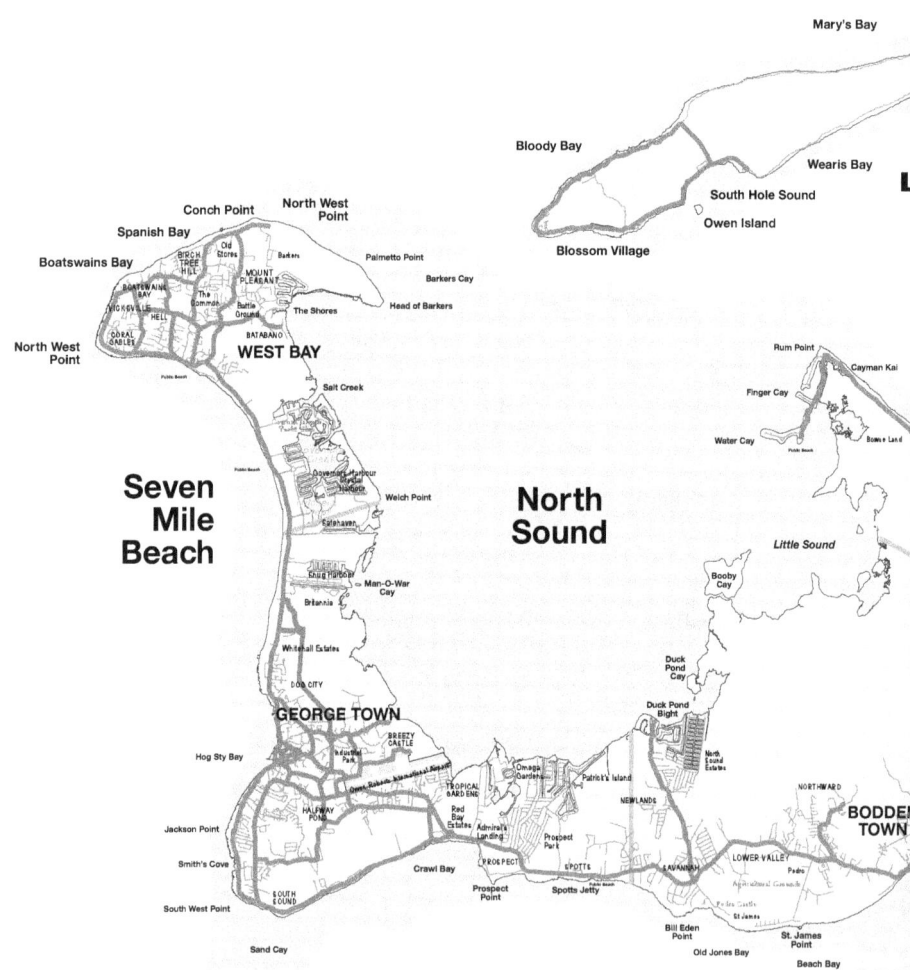

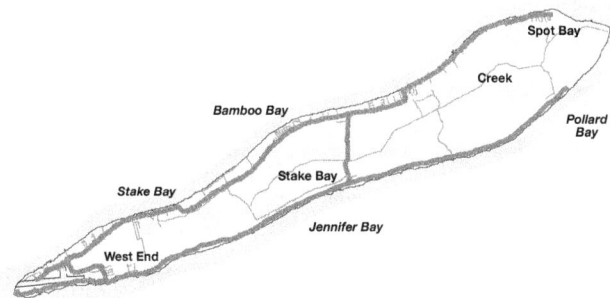

Cayman Brac

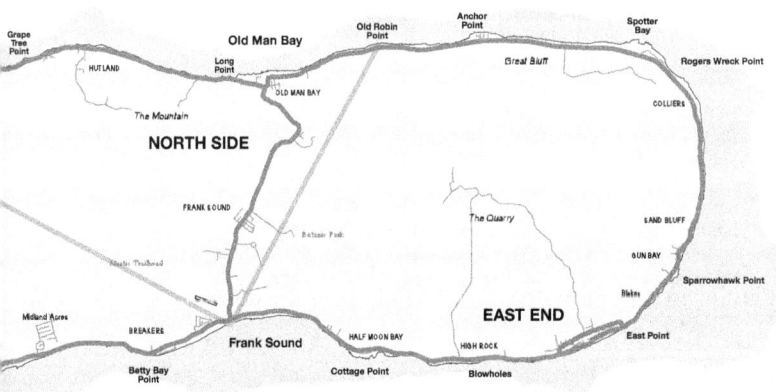

Grand Cayman

Layout copyright 2007, 2011, 2014, 2018 by Kevin M. Goring
All rights reserved. No portion of this book may be
reproduced – mechanically, electronically, or by
any other means; including photocopying,
digitizing/scanning, etc. without written permission
of the author/publisher:

Caymanology©
P.O. Box 1142
Grand Cayman KY1-1101
Cayman Islands
Email: info@caymanology.com
Official Website: www.caymanology.com

The Cayman Islands Dictionary©
A Collection of Words used by Native Caymanians
(from the Caymanology© Collection)
Design and Layout by Kevin M. Goring
Compiled and Written by Kevin M. Goring
Chief Editor: Sarah V. Goring
Copy Editors/Proofreaders: Kurt Goring, Leticia Goring
Contributors: Tania Ebanks, Avons Ebanks,
Inez Goring, Ted Goring
Copyright registered 27 April 2007 and updated 8 July 2008
Printed in the USA
Limited Special Edition printed November 2011.
Limited International Edition printed November 2018.
Amazon ISBN: 9781790343676

All words and phrases contained in this presentation
have been drawn from authentic sources, including books,
interviews, references, the Cayman Islands National Archive
(eg. bush med'sin, crabbin', donkey man, balboa, cimboco, etc.),
the media-at-large, etc. and are not necessarily the views of
the author nor its contributors.

Every effort has been made to present all information
accurately. No liability is accepted for any inclusions or
advice given or for omissions from the publication.
GapSeed and the Author of *The Cayman Islands Dictionary©*
are not liable for any information that may have been
misrepresented by third parties during the research process.

LIMITED INTERNATIONAL EDITION

★ ★ ★ ★ ★

THE CAYMAN ISLANDS DIC·TION·ARY

A COLLECTION OF WORDS USED BY NATIVE CAYMANIANS

Compiled and Written by
KEVIN M. GORING

A QUICK GUIDE TO
Caymanian Words

Caymanians are a proud people with a rich cultural history that has been passed on for generations through persistent communication of our linguistic heritage. Our dialect consists of countless words and phrases that are often pronounced with a variety of unique accents which tend to vary by district. It is also one of the most intriguing aspects of the Caymanian culture that visitors enjoy during their time on the Islands and we are always happy to share this with the world.

Therefore, for the edification of all first-time readers, we have provided the following list of basic words that are used by natives throughout the Islands on a daily basis. Feel free to refer to it when necessary as it will certainly enhance the pleasure of reading this book. Enjoy!

Awright	Alright	**Ih'nah**	You know
Beliewe	Believe	**N'**	And
B'long	Belong	**Nah**	Not
Bug/'Bout	About	**Nuttin'**	Nothing
Cyah	Can't	**Ol'**	Old
Cyar	Carry	**'Rong**	Around
Dah	That	**Ta/Tuh**	To
Dat	That	**Urr**	Our
Diss	This	**Waugh**	Want
Doon'	Don't	**Wuh/Wah**	What/Was
Ereckleh	Later	**Yih**	You
Fuh/Fa	For	**Yih'nah**	You know
Gye'n	Going	**Yoh**	Your

Ackee (ah-kih) *Noun* – **1.** *Blighia sapida;* a tropical Caribbean evergreen tree having leathery red and yellow fruits. It is naturalized and cultivated in the tropics and in Florida. **2.** the edible, fleshy, ripe aril of this tree, especially popular as a food in the Cayman Islands. **Eg.** *"Anytime yah waugh sump'm good ta eat, juss try some Ackee n' Codfish from Miss Vivine Kitchen. She kin cook good y'see!"*

Ackee Stick (ah-kih stik) *Noun* – **1.** a long stick designated for picking Ackees. **2.** a fruit-picking instrument which is generally shorter than a *breadfruit stick* and much thinner than a *mango stick*. **Eg.** *"Henry go find my ackee stick so I kin pick sum fa dinna nah?"*

Ackee Tree Garage (ah-kih tree gah-radj) *Noun* – **1.** a 'small-time garage'. **2.** a private business which involves one or two mechanics working on cars under an actual ackee tree, or similar trees. **3.** the poor man's alternative to using a professional mechanic. **Eg.** *"Doon' mek nobody from ah ackee tree garage touch yoh car unless you know fah sure dey know wah dey doin'."*

Acks (Ahks) *Verb* – **1.** to solicit (ask). **2.** to make a formal or informal request. **Eg.** *"I hate hawin' ta acks my boss fah anyting cuz he always be in ah bad mood."*

Agouti (ah-goo-tee) *Noun* – **1.** the Cayman jackrabbit. **2.** any of several short-haired, short-eared, rabbit-like rodents of the genus *Dasyprocta* of South and Central America and the West Indies; destructive to sugar cane. **Eg.** *"If you tink you fass, try ketch ah agouti wit yoh bare hands. Dem lil' tings run like lightnin' yih'nah!"*

Aa

Agriculcha Field (ahg'reh kull-chah feel) *Noun* – **1.** the property on which the current Cricket Field is located. **2.** the venue for the annual Agricultural Show during the 1980s and early 1990s. **3.** a popular site for football games during the 1980s. **Eg.** *"Maannn, I kin rememba when I used ta watch Renard Moxam n' Dale Ramoon shiffin' up all kinda man up by Agriculcha Field."*

Ah Good Lil' While (ah guud lill wyle) *Slang* – **1.** some time ago. **2.** a pretty long time, but not too long. **Eg.** *"I doon' know wah Kurtis be doin' in dah bahtchroom but he bin in deh fah ah good lil' while n' I needa get ready fa work."*

Ah Lil' (ah -lill) *Interjection* – **1.** a non-specific reference to something large or small, depending on the object and the occasion. **3.** a common expression of amazement. **Eg.** *"Look yah! Ah lil' car he gah deh. Dah ting barely look like it gah ah engine!"*

Ah Pretty (ah prih-deh) *Adverb* – **1.** silly. **2.** ludicrous, foolish, goofy. **3.** ridiculous. *Noun* – **4.** a type of marble. **Eg.** *"Cuzzy, hear wah I tell you, if you go up in dah Maiden Plum Bush, when you come out you gah look ah pretty, n' I nah tennin' ta ya nydah"*

Ahn (aah'n) *Noun* – **1.** one's aunt. **2.** the sister of one's father or mother. **3.** the wife of one's uncle. **4.** someone to love or fear when your parents are not around. **Eg.** *"Lisa, go so acks ya Ahn Dean if you kin sleep ova her house t'night cuz I gah go church."*

Ahn'deh (aah'n-deh) *Noun* – **1.** one's aunt. **2.** the sister of one's father or mother. **3.** the wife of one's uncle. **4.** someone to love or fear when your parents are not around. **Eg.** *"My ahn'deh always say if I be good she gah take me Tampa n' go shoppin.'"*

Ah Wah (ah-wah) *Suffix* – **1.** or what. **2.** the end of a question. **3.** yes or no. **Eg.** *"Morris, you goin' back home now ah wah?"* or; *"Dah you ah wah?"*

Aie! (eye) *Interjection* – **1.** wow!; woah! **2.** ouch! **3.** oh my gosh! **Eg.** *"Aie! Watch way ya goin' nah? You jess step on my toes wit dem big ol' hoofs you gah deh!"* or; *"Daddy, Daddy, No! please doon' lick me wit dah switch again, aie!"*

Aingh! (eyenghh) *Interjection* – From West Bay; **1.** take that. **2.** yes. **3.** its about time. **4.** good for you. **Eg.** *"Aingh! Tek daah! You waugh run chrew people grass piece? Ah know ya look ah pretty now wid dah horse dung all ohwah yoh new school shoes."*

Air Condition (ere kun-dih-shun) *Adjective* – **1.** having holes or full of holes. **2.** allowing passage in and out. **3.** old or tattered clothing which are full of holes, resembling a/c vents. **Eg.** *"When Clinton had rip he pants, errybody say it wah air-condition cuz it wah rip from front ta back."*

Ajiculcha Show Ground (ah-jih-kul-chuh sho groun) *Noun* – **1.** the former Agricultural Field, currently known as the Cricket Field which is located on Thomas Russell Way; near Owen Roberts International Airport. **Eg.** *"I doon' know how come u doon' rememba goin' ta Family Fair Day up by Ajiculcha Show Ground. Dah wah so much fun!"*

Allawow (ah-lah-wow) *Interjection* – From Old People Times; **1.** to express one's surprise or dismay. **2.** to become excited. **3.** caught off guard. **4.** to be amazed. **Eg.** *"Allawow! Ya almost mek me jump outta my skin!"*

All Channels (awl chah'nulz) *Noun* – **1.** one of Cayman's early movie rental facilities which specialized in pre-recorded Beta and VHS tapes. All Channels was located at Merren's Plaza near the Watler's Road area of George Town. **Eg.** *"Erry Satday my whole family used ta go All Channels n' rent one whole pile ah moowiz boy."*

All Deck Out (awll dek owt) *Adverb* – **1.** dressed more formally or elaborately than necessary. **2.** dressed up. **3.** impressively adorned with clothing. **4.** very dapper. **Eg.** *"When MC Hammer wah popula I used ta go by Faces Niteclub all deck out in my parachute pants n' ting."*

Alloways (ah-loh-waze) *Noun* – **1.** *Aloacae*; any aloe of the species *Aloe Vera* which originated in the Canary Islands. **2.** a puss-like liquid from the aloe vera plant which is sometimes used to reprimand children who use foul language. (also known as: **semper vivie, simpa wiwie,** or **aloe wera**) **Eg.** *"Ttry hush yoh mout in church t'day or else daddy gah mek ya drink ah whole bottle ah alloways."*

Aa

American Football (ah-mear-ih-kun Futboll) *Noun* – **1.** an Americanized version of the sport of Rugby. **2.** Cayman's way of distinguishing the American sport from the world-standard sport of 'Football'. **3.** a word that is openly disputed by many Caymanians for causing unnecessary confusion. **Eg.** *"Wheneva Robert be down in he American Football he doon' pay nobody mind."*

And Odd (in awd) *Conjunction* – **1.** and more. **2.** more than the current figure. **3.** the prime number plus an unknown number. **4.** an unknown figure. **5.** into the unknown. **Eg.** *"Really n' truly, if I had know dah private dentist woulda charge me five hundred and odd dollas fah ah fillin', I woulda jess gone hospital."*

And Someting (in sum-teeng) *Conjunction* – **1.** and whatever else. **2.** more than what is currently known. **3.** the prime figure plus an unknown amount. **4.** an unknown figure. **Eg.** *"Me n' my wife just paid 'bout ah tousin' and someting dollas fah uwah plane tickets ta Disney World."*

Annex (ah-nix) *Noun* – **1.** Cayman's most popular football arena, located between School House Road and Eastern Avenue. **2.** the George Town playing field. **3.** the football pitch adjacent to the George Town Primary school. **Eg.** *"I 'memba dah Sundeh affanoon when Scholars had beat Strikers down by Annex."*

Any n' Errybody (eh-neh-in-eh-reh-baw-deh) *Noun* – **1.** any person at all; anybody. **2.** anyone. **3.** whomever. **Eg.** *"I doon' know how some people kin still put dey clothes on da line fa any n' errybody ta see."*

Any Ol' How (eh-neh-ole-hou) *Adverb* – **1.** any how. **2.** any way whatever. **3.** in any case; at all events. **4.** in a careless manner; haphazardly. **5.** at any rate. **Eg.** *"I cyah teck da way dem mobile car wash people do my car yih'see? Dey juss like ta wipe it up any ol' how n' expeck people ta satisfy wit waheva dey gi um."*

Areckleh (ah-reck-leh) *Adverb* – **1.** later. **2.** the not-so-distant future. **3.** a future time to come. (also pronounced: **'ereckleh'**, **'dereckleh'**, or **'tereckleh'** in some areas) **Eg.** *"Sometimes it bedda ta know wah ya dealin' wit right now dun tah fine out 'areckleh'."*

Aa

[Ol'] Arnold (ole ar-null) *Noun* – **1.** a local crow, bearing dark-coloured feathers and parrot-like features. **Eg.** *"Dah ol' Arnold cyah stop mekkin' nize while I tryin' sleep ah wah?"*

Awleh (awe-leh) *Interjection* – From West Bay; **1.** a startled reaction to a particular situation. **2.** a verbal demonstration of surprise. **3.** another way of saying "oh my gosh!" **4.** reference to a group of individuals. **Eg.** *"Awleh! I didd'n know you could fishin' like dah."* or; *"Awleh unna come less go wid me ta da supamahkit."*

Awlehkipitins (awe-leh-kipp-eh-tinz) *Interjection* – From 'Old People Times'; **1.** a general expression of excitement or dismay. **2.** another way of saying 'Are you serious' or; 'Really?'. **Eg.** *"Awlehkipitins! I cyah beliewe I didd'n rememba ta bring my false teet ta church! I cyah sing widdout 'um yih'nah."*

Awlehmillikins (awe-leh-mih-lih-kinz) *Interjection* – From 'Old People Times'; **1.** a general expression of excitement or dismay. **2.** another way of saying 'Oh my gosh!' **3.** wow! **Eg.** *"Awlehmilikins! Deez people newah learn how ta drive before dey get dey license a wah?"*

Aw'right (awh-rite) *Adverb* – **1.** without doubt (used to reinforce assertion); *"aw'right nah, jess lee me alone"* **2.** an expression of agreement normally occurring at the beginning of a sentence. **Eg.** *"Da new Turtle Farm dat juss build look kinda aw'right, but it cost too much money man."*

Awh-Awh! (Augh-Auwwhhh) *Interjection* – **1.** an expression of disappointment or unexpected surprise. **Eg.** *"Awh-awh! Boy look yah. If you doon' get outta my room I gah tell daddy on you."*

Aye (aay) *Interjection* – **1.** hey. **2.** you. **3.** a verbal gesture or signal to attract attention. **4.** the first word in an angry sentence. **Eg.** *"Aye you lil' boy, you cyah hear stay outta people yard ah wah?"*

Ayegah (aay-gah) *Adjective* – **1.** feverish. **2.** pertaining to, of the nature of, or resembling fever. **3.** cold chills. **4.** excited, restless, or uncontrolled, as if from fever. **Eg.** *"Boy I dunno if I kin go movies wid unna t'night. I feel kinda ayegah n' dah a/c gah mek it worse."*

Babes (baybz) *Slang* – **1.** one's sweetheart; dear. **2.** a young woman or man. **3.** either of a pair of lovers in relation to the other. **4.** a term of endearment for one's lover. **5.** a generous, friendly person. **Eg.** *"Babes, you juss goin' bade now? We gah be late fa da movies yih'nah?"*

Backhand Slap (bak han slahpp) *Noun* – **1.** a strike to the face using the rear of one's hand. **2.** a stroke, slap, etc., made with the back of the hand turned in the direction of the stroke, slap, etc. **Eg.** *"If you doon' stop yoh fassniss, I gah gi ya one backhand slap so hard yoh mama gah feel it."*

Back House (bak howce) *Noun* – **1.** an old Cayman-style bathroom made of wood, built over a large pit, which houses one or more crudely made toilet seats. **Eg.** *"I used ta hate goin' ta my granny's cuz all she had wah ah back house n' I always use ta get stuck in deh wit no tylit paper."*

Backin' News (bak-in nyuwze) *Verb* – **1.** gossiping. **2.** engaged in idle talk or rumor, esp. about the personal or private affairs of others. **3.** to share in small talk, hearsay, palaver, chitchat. **Eg.** *"Erry election time people be backin' all kinda news 'bout dem MLA's yih'see."*

Bad Luckid (bah'd luh-kidd) *Adjective* – **1.** cursed; doomed. **2.** stricken with misfortune. **Eg.** *"Lemme hold dem eggs cuz you so bad luckid you mite drop um."*

Bald Forrid (ball-foh-rid) *Noun* – **1.** *bald forehead*; a large and hairless area of the forehead which recedes into the hairline. **Eg.** *"Dey say if ya wear hats too much yih get bald forrid early n' look like ah ol' man."*

Bb

Bammy (bah-mih) *Noun* – **1.** a must have for traditional Caymanian families as it is often eaten with fish and other dishes. **2.** a Cassava bread which is generally baked and eaten with meat during Christmas time. **Eg.** *"My Granny conch stew n' bammy taste like angels had cook it."*

Barra (bah-rah) *Noun* – **1.** the great, fearsome, Barracuda; ray-finned fishes notable for their large size and fearsome appearance. The body is long, fairly compressed, and covered with small, smooth scales. **Eg.** *"Gillis tell me det one time when he wah spear fishin' one Barra had chase im right out da wadda; all up on one reef in East End, yih'nah."*

Basley (baz-leh) *Noun* – **1.** *Basil*; any of several aromatic herbs belonging to the genus *Ocimum*, of the mint family, as *O. basilicum* (sweet basil), having purplish-green ovate leaves used in cooking. **2.** an aromatic shrubby plant. **Eg.** *"I like how Cimboco use basley on dey pizza yih'see?"*

Baw-Baw (bawh bawh) *Slang* – **1.** a baby's bottle. **2.** a bottle with a teat (or nipple) to drink directly from. **3.** the easiest way to satisfy a young baby when one is tired of breastfeeding. **Eg.** *"My sweetums, ya waugh ya baw-baw now nah? Doon' worry, mummy soon have it ready."*

Baya (bay-ah) *Noun* – **1.** an individual who was born in the district of West Bay. **Eg.** *"If yah waugh know 'bout good fishnin' juss acks any Baya n' dey kin tell ya way ta go."*

Beady Head (bee-deh hed) *Noun* – **1.** having small beadlike hair clusters in one's head due to lack of grooming. **2.** short curly hair that is nearly impossible and extremely painful to comb. **Eg.** *"Boy you bedda try buy 10 gallons ah shampoo ta get ridda dah ol' beady head."*

Beggin' Bread (bay-gin bred) *Adjective* – **1.** torn apart, ragged, open, exposed. **2.** having a huge gaping hole in the front of an old shoe which exposes the toes to onlookers. **Eg.** *"One time when Ornel had wear he church shoes ta football, aftawurds he shoes wah beggin' bread."*

Big Finga (big fee'ng-gah) *Noun* – **1.** one's thumb. **2.** the short, thick, inner digit of the human hand next to the forefinger. **Eg.** *"Mahma, I juss jam my big finga in da door. You gah any ban-daids?"*

Big Hard Back Man (big hah'rd bak-mahn) *Noun* – **1.** a grown man of 30 years or older who is generally hard-working and respected for being independent; inspirational. **Eg.** *"Come now, you know ah big hard back man like you nah suppose tah live up in bar room."*

Big Odd (big awd) *Conjunction* – **1.** a huge unknown amount. **2.** more than what was expected. **3.** a lot more than one should have to pay for anything. **4.** too much. **Eg.** *"I gah hahwe walk rong bare foot, cuz deez people chargin' ah hundred n' big odd dollas juss fa two lil' shoes."*

Bird Chest (burd chess) *Noun* – **1.** the upper torso area of a lean-bodied male which often lacks muscularity. **2.** the underdeveloped chest area of a growing teenage boy or young man. **Eg.** *"I doon' like changin' afta football practice cuz errybody always say dey doon' waugh see my bird chest."*

Blue Iguana (bloo ee-gwawh-nuh) *Noun* – **1.** *Cyclura nubile lewesi*; the indigineous species of iguana which has become endangered due to the growth and development of the Cayman Islands. **2.** one the Cayman Islands' many National Symbols. **Eg.** *"Bobo, ya bedda nah mek National Trust ketch you wit dah Blue Iguana cuz dey gah lock ya up n' chrow way da key."*

Bobo (boh-boh) *Pronoun* – From West Bay; **1.** a close personal friend. **2.** the object of one's affection. **3.** a woman's pet name for a boyfriend or close male friend. **Eg.** *"I gah plenty guy friends but Derrick is my bobo, boy."*

Bodda (baw-duh) *Noun* – **1.** bother; to cause frustration by way of hinderance or constant badgering. **2.** to get on one's nerves. **3.** to interrupt. **4.** to invade the personal space of another. **Eg.** *"Lissin' yah man. Doon' bodda me no more or else I gah tell my mama on you."*

Bodden Tong (baw-din tawng) *Noun* – Bodden Town; **1.** the first capital district of Grand Cayman. **2.** the district which received the most catastrophic damage during Hurricane Ivan. **3.** the area starting from Sawannah to Breakas; including, Low Walley, Pedro and Nortwurd. **Eg.** *"Years ago, I used ta ketch Bodden Tong bus from Kirk Plaza."*

Bogga Boo (bawg-ah boo) *Noun* – **1.** hardened nasal fluid or mucus. **2.** cold in the nose. **3.** particles or projectiles which originate in the nasal passage or nostrils. **Eg.** *"Sandra say she hate da way her brudda always pick he nose n' try put da bogga boo on her."*

Bore (bohre) *Verb* – **1.** to force one's way into or through a gathering of people or an obstruction. **2.** to clear a path. **Eg.** *"People call me tattle-tale cuz I had tell on Franky when he had bore ahead ah me in da lunch line."*

Bracka (brah-kah) *Noun* – **1.** any person who is native to the island of Cayman Brac. **2.** a proud individual from one of Grand Cayman's two Sister Islands. **Eg.** *"When Mona Lisa win Miss Cayman, I wah proud ta be ah Bracka boy."*

Breadfruit (brade-froot) *Noun* – **1.** a large, round, starchy fruit borne by a tree, *Artocarpus Altilis*, of the mulberry family, native to the Caribbean islands; used, baked or roasted, for food. **2.** the tree bearing this fruit. **Eg.** *"You don't eat yoh breadfruit wit salt on it ah wah?"*

Bread Kind (brade-kine) *Noun* – **1.** starchy vegetables. **2.** side orders in a traditional Caymanian meal which include; breadfruit, sweet potato, yam and cassava. **Eg.** *"I love fish, but I cyah eat it wddout no bread kind."*

Bubbies (buh-biz) *Noun, Pl.* – **1.** the chest or upper torso area of the female anatomy. **2.** a pair of instruments used for feeding young babies. **3.** an area of the female anatomy that is attractive to the opposite sex. **Eg.** *"Mama, tell Roy stop teasin' me 'bout I nah gah no bubbies…"*

Buck Toe (buk-toh) *Noun* – **1.** the result of a painful collision between one or more toes and an inanimate object. **2.** the most popular injury among young children. **Eg.** *"When I wah small, my granfadda used ta mek me wear shoes in he grass piece so I diddn' get no buck toe."*

Bugga (bug-ah) *Noun* – **1.** one who surrounds him or herself with controversy. **2.** a person deserving great misfortune, simply for being in or around mischievious company. **3.** an idiot. **Eg.** *"If I ketch dah bugga runnin' chrew my yaad again it gah be me n' him."*

Bunkey (bung-kih) *Noun* – **1.** *gluteus maximus;* the buttocks; either of the two fleshy protuberances forming the lower and back part of the trunk. **2.** the rear pelvic area of the human body. **3.** the female body part which is most attractive to Caribbean men. (also spelled: **Bonkey**) **Eg.** *"Lass night I slip dong n' nearly bust my bunkey in two."*

Bunkey Cheeks (bung-kih) *Noun* – **1.** the fleshy extension of one's backside, used primarily for sitting or resting. **2.** the butt. (see also: **Bunkey**) **Eg.** *"Aye man, moo yoh ol' bunkey cheeks outta my face!"*

Bush Med'sin (bush med-sin) *Noun* – From Old People Times; **1.** *Bush Medicine*; any series of medical concoctions or homemade remedies made from plants or vines.

Some excellent examples are:

Tea Banker – applied to boiling water to improve the appetite
Leaf of Life – leaves roasted and squeezed to produce a juice to treat coughs.
Fever Grass – tea for colds and fever
Jennifer – bark will deaden toothache
Eucalyptus – hot baths for fever
Fine Leaf Mint – tea for upset stomachs
Worry Vine – tea to clear skin from heat rash or loss of appetite
Coconut Water – to cleanse the kidneys
Mulberry & Almond Leaves – wrapped around the feet to alleviate rheumatism
Speak Nut – for increased appetite
Birch Tree Leaves, Pear and Breadfruit buds – made into a tea and taken to alleviate high blood pressure and related symptoms
Providence Mint & Dash-a-Long – made into a tea for hearing ailments
Periwinkle Leaf – made into a tea for coughs and diabetes

Eg. *"Granny always used ta have some kinda bush med'sin ta cure any pain or sickness I had when I wah small."*

Caboose (kah-buce) *Noun* – From 'Old People Times'; **1.** a make-shift wooden stove filled with sand and rocks to hold pots and frying pans. **2.** a traditional Caymanian stove, which is similar to a modern concrete barbecue grill found at most public beaches and parks. **Eg.** *"Granny say when she wah growin' up, it wah hard ta fix breakfast on ah caboose cuz errybody had waugh see wah ya wah cookin'."*

Cah-Cah (kah-kah) *Noun* – **1.** waste matter discharged from the intestines through the anus; excrement. **2.** number two. **3.** solid excretory product evacuated from the bowels [syn: **fecal matter**]. (also called: **doo-doo** or **dee-dee**) **Eg.** *"Dah wah so funny, I almost cah-cah up myself."*

Cake-Up (kayke up) *Noun* – **1.** excessive make-up. **2.** an abundance of facial cosmetics, as eye shadow or lipstick. **3.** make-up which appears to have been applied using a spray gun and a trowel. **Eg.** *"Errytime I see dah gyal, her face always be cake up even when she up in da gym."*

Calabash (kal-ah-bash) *Noun* – **1.** *Crescentia cujete*; the large fruit from the Gourd Tree, bearing a skin/rind which was often used to make bowls, dippers, water containers and other utensils during Old People Times. **2.** a large, melon-like fruit, similar to pumpkin featuring a smooth outer hide. **Eg.** *"I hear some people use ta put calabash on dey head ta line up dey hair cut."*

Calalu (kaugh-lah-loo) *Noun* – **1.** a local dish, made from a series of plants and leafy vegetables such as the water spinach. **2.** a local weed. **3.** a vegetable which is the primary ingredient in the thick soup also known as 'pepperpot'. **Eg.** *"I cyah stand da way Calalu smell when it bein' cooked sometimes, except when my ahn'deh cookin' it."*

Calavan (kal-ah-van) *Noun* – **1.** a large box made of twigs and sticks woven together, and string (the trigger) - used to trap chickens and other game. **Eg.** *"I hear dah museum even gah one ah dem ol' calavan det Mr. Early used'ta mek."*

Calipea (kah-lih-pee) *Noun* – **1.** the part of a turtle next to the lower shield, consisting of a yellowish gelatinous substance that is considered a delicacy. **2.** an edible flesh lying beneath the lower shell of a turtle. **Eg.** *"Most people seem ta like da calipea bedda dun da ress ah da meat."*

Cane Piece (kayne peece) *Noun* – **1.** a former name for the area in George Town which includes the current George Town Hospital property as well as the Templeton Pine Lakes community. **Eg.** *"I doon' know how dem people coulda live down in Cane Piece when it wah first developin'. It wah so swampy n' fulla ah pile ah miskittas."*

Cane Row (kayne row) *Noun* – **1.** a hairstyle which involves hair being plaited into rows stretching from the forehead to the base of the neck. **2.** hair braided tightly against the scalp. **Eg.** *"Cane Row is all my big sista use ta know how ta do wit my hair when we wah growin' up."*

Canoe (kuh-noo) *Noun* – **1.** a primary means of transportation throughout the Cayman Islands during the 19th and early 20th centuries. **2.** a small elongated wooden boat which was used to transport several persons and their belongings to and from various origins. **Eg.** *"I hear dem Brackas from Creek used ta use canoe ta go check dey granparents in West End long time ago."*

Car Port (kar pohrt) *Noun* – **1.** garage for one or two cars consisting of a flat roof supported on poles. **2.** any facility which is attached to a house for the use of covering automobiles. **3.** the best place to keep tools and old junk. **Eg.** *"Ol' Fred gah all kinda fishin' lines n' old tools in he car port juss sittin' deh ketchin' duss!."*

Cartoon Box (kar-toon bawkz) *Noun* – **1.** a box or container made from thick cardboard or coated paper. **2.** a cardboard or plastic box used typically for storage or shipping. **Eg.** *"It kine ah intresstin' how Jackie Chan n' dem use cartoon box fah stunts instead ah ah real crash pad."*

Cassawa (kah-sah-wah) *Noun* – **1.** any of several tropical American plants belonging to the genus *Manihot*, of the spurge family, as *M. esculenta* (bitter cassava) and *M. dulcis* (sweet cassava), cultivated for their tuberous roots, which yield important food products. **2.** a nutritious starch from the roots, the source of tapioca. **3.** the primary ingredient in Cassava Cake. **Eg.** *"Yam Cake is awright but nuttin' cyah beat my granny Cassawa Cake."*

Cassawa Cake (kah-sah-vah kayke) *Noun* – **1.** one of Cayman's famed 'heavy cakes', which is made from the Cassava root. **2.** a tasty cake which is thick, sweet and contains ingredients which are meant to last a long time. **Eg.** *"Dem people from Scranton mecks Cassawa Cakes so good it almost meck ya waugh bite ya fingas off."*

Catboat (k'yat bote) *Noun* – **1.** a small double-ended sailboat used for turtling. **3.** a broad-beamed sailboat carrying a single sail on a mast stepped well forward and often fitted with a centerboard. **4.** a small sailboat which measures approx. twelve to thirty feet in length and could cost anywhere from six to seventy pounds sterling. **5.** a boat which was always painted blue to blend with the water and trimmed in black or white. **Eg.** *"When Papa Jim had tell me 'bug dah time he fall outta he catboat 15 miles out ta sea, I could'n beliewe when he say he wuz'n scared."*

Cat Tail (kyat tale) *Noun* – **1.** *Acalypha hispida*; the Chinille plant. **2.** a species of the Chinille plant which blooms almost every day of the year and produces long flowers that supposedly feel like the fabric 'chenille' and resemble a (red) cat's tail. **3.** a really beautiful plant which produces a reddish coloured flower that resembles a cat's tail. **Eg.** *"Mama, Miss Ivy waugh fine out if you kin ketch piece ah Cat Tail so gi her ta put in her yaad."*

Cayman (kay-mahn) *Noun* – **1.** a British Overseas Territory which was discovered in 1503 when one of Christopher Columbus' ships became lost during a storm. **2.** three tropical islands located 480 miles south of Florida. The Islands have had many names on maps and documents, including; *Las Tortugas* – the turtles (used by Columbus); *Las Yslas de los Latargos* – islands of the lizards; *Caymanas* – derived from the Carib word for crocodile, was first used on a chart around 1530. – Various spellings of the word Cayman on maps and documents include; *Caimanos; Keimanos; Caiman; Caimanes; Caymanns; Key of Manus*. The Lesser Islands (Sister Islands) were identified as: *Cayman Chicos; los Caymanes; Petit Camanis; Camanbrack; Cayman Breccia*. **3.** any of various tropical American crocodilians of the genus *Caiman* and related genera, resembling and closely related to the alligators. **Eg.** *"Chile, nobody bedda nah say nuttin' bad 'bout Cayman or else it gah be me n' dem cuz diss my lil' piece ah rock."*

Caymanas (kay-mah-nuz) *Noun* – **1.** the Carib word for the marine crocodile, which was abundant in the Cayman Islands in 1670. **2.** the second recorded name for the Cayman Islands, whose first name (Las Tortugas) was given by Christopher Columbus in 1503, when he discovered the two Sister Islands. **Eg.** *"I doon' waugh hear nuttin' bout no Tortugas and no Caymanas. We name Cayman Islands now so try leave da past in da past."*

Cayman Brac Bread (kay-mahn brack bred) *Noun* – **1.** a very tasty bread which comes from the Sister Island of Cayman Brac. **2.** a bread which is highly coveted by Grand Caymanians. **3.** real traditional homestyle bread. **Eg.** *"Boy I lowe ah Cayman Brac bread. Erry time I go deh, I gah bring back one or two juss fa me n' some fa my fam'leh."*

Caymania (kay-mah-ny'ah) *Noun* – From Old People Times; **1.** the *SS Caymania*; a vessel which was originally bought to replace the *Cimboco* in 1946, which served as a cargo vessel between Jamaica, Tampa and the Cayman Islands. **2.** a 60 passenger yacht which was originally known as the 'Black Bear' and owned by the Singer Sewing Machine Company. **3.** one the most beautiful boats the Islands had ever seen at the time, which was a welcomed sight to Cayman residents. **Eg.** *"I really can't rememba much 'bout da Caymania, but dey say it wah like watchin' ah angel floatin' on da sea."*

Caymanian (kay-mahn-yun) *Noun* – **1.** an individual who was born in one of the three Cayman Islands. **2.** one of several thousand people who became a Caymanian through parentage or grants of status for other reasons. **3.** one who has been naturalized as a citizen of the Cayman Islands. **Eg.** *"Dah time when I went Alaska, I taut I wan dreamin' when I saw ah Caymanian feedin' da whales!"*

Caymanian Caymanian (kay-mahn-yun kay-mahn-yun) *Noun* – **1.** a special emphasis used to define a person who was born and raised in the Cayman Islands and has a significant amount of family heritage (eg. at least one parent who has two or more preceding generations of ancestry). **3.** a full Caymanian by birthright and family lineage. **Eg.** *"I know dah boy by face, but tell me someting? He 'Caymanian Caymanian' or he juss raise up yah? Sometimes yih cyah tell n' I doon' like ta be rong."*

Caymanite (kay-mahn-nite) *Noun* – **1.** a rare semi-precious stone found only in the Cayman Islands. **2.** a composite of various precious metals and fossils. **3.** a sedimentary rock composed of narrow layers of various colours and usually found between thick deposits of white limestone. some of the layers are nearly as hard as quartz. **Eg.** *"When I get my house fix up I gah try get ah nice caymanite statue ta put in my livin' room."*

Caymanize (kay-mahn-eyze) *Verb* – **1.** to incorporate into the Cayman way of doing things. **2.** to make *'Caymanian'*. **3.** to localize. **4.** adapt for use in Cayman. **Eg.** *"Sometimes if tings doon' wuk out da way yah want it ya juss gah try Caymanize it so people kin undastand."*

Caymanology (kay-mahn-awe-loh-jeh) *Noun* – **1.** the study, preservation and promotion of all things 'Caymanian'. Its primary objective is to educate, entertain, inspire and empower Caymanians and to promote Caymanian culture to non-Caymanian residents and visitors. **2.** a brand of Cayman-inspired products. **3.** a Pro-Caymanian campaign to enrich the culture of the Cayman Islands through the development of its indigenous people. **Eg.** *"I taut 'Caymanology' wah juss books, but it ah whole pile ah tings det nah eeb'm come out yet."*

Caymanopoly (kay-mahn-op-a-leh) *Noun* – **1.** a Caymanized version of the popular board game known as *'Monopoly'*. **2.** a board game which was first developed by the Junior Achievement program in the early 1990s. **3.** an excellent souvenir for tourists and locals alike. **Eg.** *"Erry year Junior Achievement used ta mek some serious dollas sellin' dem Caymanopoly games ta tourisses."*

Cayman Parrot (kay-mahn pah-rut) *Noun* – **1.** an indigineous, yet nearly extinct species of parrot which inhabits the Cayman Islands. **2.** one of only two thousand of the same species of parrot in existence in the Cayman Islands. **3.** a beautiful green and yellow bird, which bears a red-orange mask. **4.** the Cayman Islands' National Bird. **Eg.** *"I need ah nice pitcha ow ah Cayman Parrot so I kin puddit tup in my liwin' room when I bill my house."*

Cayman Ridge (kay-mahn ridj) *Noun* – **1.** a range of submarine mountains continuous with the *Sierra Misteriosa* range of Cuba and running west in the direction of British Honduras (Belize). **Eg.** *"doon' try go scuba divin' by yo'self ova da Cayman Ridge."*

Cayman Time (kay-mahn tyme) *Noun* – **1.** at least 10mins. to 1hr. past the reasonable time for any meeting or function to begin. **2.** expected delays. **3.** a common excuse for being late. **4.** an alibi for tardiness **Eg.** *"Any reggae show ya go to in Cayman dey always be startin' on Cayman time so I jess go layda den wah da flya say."*

Cayman Trench (kay-mahn trehn'ch) *Noun* – **1.** a submarine trench of the floor of the Caribbean Sea between the Cayman Islands and Jamaica. **2.** the area also known as the *Bartlett Trench* or *Bartlett Trough*. **3.** one of the deepest parts of the Caribbean sea, measuring just over 25,000 feet in depth **Eg.** *"I hear one time some Cubians had fall ova board ova da Cayman Trench tryin' reach Cayman."*

Cayman Wall (kay-man wohl) *Noun* – **1.** a steep submarine cliff which drops to 3,200 feet, (three miles) offshore. **2.** a popular dive destination for scuba divers, skin divers, and research submersibles. **3.** one of Cayman's main tourist attractions. **Eg.** *"Bobo, if you doon' stop messin' wit me, I gah cyar you out by da Cayman Wall n' pitch you ovaboard."*

Chah (ch'ah) *Interjection* – **1.** a verbal release of inner tension. **2.** an expression of disappointment and/or frustration. **3.** this is ridiculous. **4.** what-in-the-world? **Eg.** *"Nah-nah! You cyah see I wah watchin' cricket ah wah? Chah! Try moo frum yah n' go back way'eva you come out frum. Always gah fass wit people tings wen it nah yohs."*

Chafe Up (chay'f upp) *Adverb* – **1.** painful from having the skin abraded. *Noun* – **3.** an affliction which is common among bicycle riders, due to constant rubbing against the seat, and also occurs in babies, due to moisture and friction inside the pampers. **Eg.** *"Aaron say afta he had finish wit dah bike-ah-ton lass week he wah so chafe up he hadda rub all kine ah lotion between he legs jess ta walk straight."*

Checkin' (chek in) *Verb* – **1.** the second stage in the four-part structure of a relationship, which involves: *1. talkin' 2. checkin' 3. dealin' 4. goin'*. **2.** courting. **3.** the dating era of an uncommitted relationship. **Eg.** *"Lacey say if I doon' hurry up n' decide wah I doin' she gah tell errybody we nah checkin' no more."*

Cheesy Foot (chee-zeh fuh't) *Noun* – **1.** an extremely smelly foot or pair of feet, due to sweat and dirt. **2.** stink feet. **Eg.** *"Aye! Get yoh ol' cheesy foot off me man! It smell like bun up Doritoes."*

Cheesy Socks (chee-zeh socks) *Noun* – **1.** any pair of socks which have been worn long enough to smell like sweat and dirt. **2.** toe jam central. **3.** stink socks. **Eg.** *"Felicia, ya brudda say muss come get yoh cheesy socks outta he bedroom fa he set um on fiyah."*

Cheesy Toes (chee-zeh toze) *Noun* – **1.** toe jam. **2.** any material that collects between the toes. **3.** the remains of sweat, dirt and fluids which settle between the toes. **4.** a strong odor which fills the room after removing ones shoes. **Eg.** *"If it's one ting ta say 'bout Franklin', I kin surely say he gah da rottenest cheesy toes I ehwah smell in my life."*

Chimmy (chih-meh) *Noun* – **1.** a small round pot used for collecting urine and fecal matter. **2.** an early toilet. **3.** a large metal bowl. **Eg.** *"Afta Iwan, I hadda mek ah chimmy outta ah ol' chair n' ah 5 gallon pail."*

Chimmy Days (chih-meh daze) *Noun* – **1.** Old People Times. **2.** An early part of the 20th Century when it was normal for people to use portable metal or ceramic utensils as toilets. **3.** An era of humble upbringings. **Eg.** *"My granny say durin' her chimmy days, people neva used ta be spiteful like t'day."*

Ching-Ching (ching-ching) *Noun* – **1.** the common Cayman black bird. **2.** a bird which scavenges on garbage and other other unwanted food. **3.** a real nuisance. **4.** one of the most common birds which when trapped inside a building, is virtually impossible to get out. **Eg.** *"One day one Ching-Ching took ah dump in my friend head."*

Choong Gum (chyoong'h gumm) *Noun* – **1.** chewing gum. **2.** a sweetened and flavored preparation for chewing, usually made of chicle. **Eg.** *"Sweetie, nex time when yah go CoMart's bring meh back some choong gum nah?"*

Chroo (ch'roo) *Adjective* – **1.** true. **2.** in accordance with the actual state or conditions; conforming to reality or fact; not false; a true story. **3.** sincere; not deceitful. **4.** legitimate or rightful. **Eg.** *"If it chroo wah you say, I gah string up Angie Lee if I ketch her with Rodney again."*

Chrute (ch'root) *Adjective* – **1.** the truth, or actual state of a matter. **2.** in accordance with the actual state or conditions; conforming to reality or fact; not false; the honest chrewt. **3.** conformity with fact or reality; verity. **4.** the legitimacy of known facts. **Eg.** *"If ya doon' believe wah I sayin' jess acks Rodney, n' he kin tell yah da chrute."*

Church Clothes (chirch klohz) *Noun, Pl.* – **1.** formal clothing that is purchased with the specific intention of being worn only to church. **2.** an assortment of formal clothing and shoes. **Eg.** *"Even doh Mena is only 12, she look like ah big woman wheneva she got on her church clothes."*

Cimboco (sim-boh-koh) *Noun* – **1.** one of the first schooners built by Caymanian shipwright, Captain Rayal Brazley Bodden. **2.** a 120ft. vessel, built in a George Town shipyard and launched for the first time in 1927. **3.** a popular local restaurant which is currently located in the Marquee Plaza, and named after the popular schooner. **4.** the first locally-owned motorship, wich was named after the company that owned her, the *Cayman Islands Motor Boat Company* (whose President was Dr. Roy McTaggart). The Cimboco was sold to the Archibold Brothers of Columbia in 1947. **Eg.** *"I nehwa new dat Cimboco was ah boat. I always taught it wah juss da name ah restaurant."*

Clean Out (kleen owt) *Adjective* – **1.** an old wives solution to any illness. **2.** of, pertaining to, or constituting a laxative; purgative. **3.** to enduce bowel movement by consuming a laxative or a traditional sursee concoction. **Eg.** *"Erry summa when we wah growin' up, my mama hadda gi us ah good clean out b'fore school start back."*

Cochineal (koh-cheh-neel) *Noun* – **1.** one of the many species of medicinal plants (better known as 'bush med'sin), which has various uses. **2.** a form of cactus, of which the inside pulp was used (during Old People Times) as a shampoo and hair conditioner and also to treat wounds. **Eg.** *"Granny say she doon' care nuttin' bug no 'Head n' Shouldas' but it gah hawe do cuz dey doon' use cochineal ta wash ya hair no more."*

Coco Plum (kuh-kuh plum) *Noun* – **1.** a small yellow fruit with a white, meaty inside, which is thick, slightly slippery, and can be tartish in taste. **2.** a small fruit tree which grows primarily near the ocean, but can be found near other bodies of water including ponds. **Eg.** *"Boy, I wish I had ah Coco Plum tree in my yaad doh yih'nah."*

Cold Chills (cole chih'lz) *Noun* – **1.** a sensation of coldness, often accompanied by shivering and pallor of the skin. **2.** an abnormal condition of the body, characterized by undue depression in temperature, lagging of the pulse, and disturbance of various body functions. **Eg.** *"Hot Tea wit Lime is da bess ting ta get rid ah Cold Chills any day."*

Cold Front (koal'd frunt) *Noun* – **1.** the transition zone where a cold air mass is replacing a warmer air mass. *cold fronts* generally move from northwest to southeast. **2.** a seemingly valid reason for Caymanians to break out full winter clothes and behave as if they are in Aspen. **Eg.** *"Wheneva ah cold front pass chrew Cayman I always feel like I walkin' round New York wit my bubble jacket n' tam."*

Coldy Nose (koal-eh noze) *Noun* – **1.** having clogged nostrils during illness; such as, with a common cold or flu. **2.** excessive fluid in the nostril region. **3.** runny nose. **4.** stuffy nose. **Eg.** *"If you doon' waugh see my coldy nose; look someway else den."*

Colliers (kawl-yerz) *Pronoun* – **1.** the East End community located between Gun Bay and Old Man Bay. **2.** the area of East End where Morritt's Tortuga Club is located. **3.** a great place to watch the sun come up in the morning. **Eg.** *"Dah time when Wilfred had get he leg break, yih could hear 'im screamin' all da way in Colliers."*

Conch Shell Blowin' (cunk sheh'l bloh-win) *Verb* – **1.** the art of sounding an alarm or signal from arriving fishermen to alert the area as to whether they were carrying fish to trade or sell. **2.** the technique used in sounding a traditional Caymanian horn of which (when blown) the sound travels a great distance to welcome buyers and sellers to the market. **Eg.** *"My gran-fadda use ta practice he conch shell blowin' erry weekend n' sometimes it use ta fool people inta tinkin' it wah da fishamen."*

Cook'nut (cook-nut) *Noun* – **1.** the coconut. **2.** the large, hard-shelled seed of the coconut tree lined with a white edible meat and containing a milky fluid. **Eg.** *"One day when my brudda wah walkin' rong da back ah da house, he hear one tump on da roof n' when he look, one cook'nut land right in he chest. I know dah mussa hurt!"*

Cook'nut Meat (cook'nut meet) *Noun* – **1.** the edible white meat of a coconut; often shredded for use in cakes and curries. **2.** one of two favourite parts of a coconut. **3.** a Caymanian delicacy. **Eg.** *"I hear Craft Market sellin' cook'nut meat fa ah dolla ah bag."*

Cook Rum (kook ruhm) *Noun* – From Old People Times; **1.** a 'Cooking Room'; a large detatched building (almost) as big as the main house and connected by a 'tramway' or wooden walk, where the fire hearth was kept. **2.** a traditional Caymanian kitchen, which was detatched from the main house, due to the heat of the cooking. **3.** the place where the 'caboose' (an early wooden-box oven filled with sand) was kept. **4.** a detatched building, built to protect the main house from fires, which would happen occasionally when the caboose would overheat. **Eg.** *"Dah time when Ol' Fred cook rum ketch on fiyah all kine ah people wah bailin' wadda from he cistern ta try out it."*

Cc

Cool Out (kool owt) *Verb* – **1.** to relax. **2.** forget about all of one's worries. **3.** an activity which brings about great joy and peace of mind. **4.** to make less tense, rigid, or firm. **5.** to find a spot in the shade, hang a hammock and rest. **6.** take a nap in the shade. **Eg.** *"Rum Point beach is da bess place in Cayman ta sit back, orda some food n' juss cool out."*

Corn Fish (kawrn fish) *Pronoun* – **1.** a cooking recipe for fish, which is first salted and then hung out to dry thoroughly. **2.** a traditional Cayman meal which often resembles cooked codfish. **Eg.** *"I hate da smell ah corn fish but it taste good doh."*

Corn Turtle (korn tur-tul) *Adverb* – **1.** a process of marinating turtle meat, which involves salting prior to storage in several barrels. once marinated, the meat is taken out and stewed as needed. **2.** a treatment of turtle meat which looks like corned beef when cooked. **Eg.** *"If yah get some good corn turtle deez daze, ya bedda bite yah finga off eatin' it cuz yih nah gah see it again no time soon."*

Cotters (kaw-terz) *Pronoun* – **1.** a traditional hairstyle created by rolling one's hair into small clumps and fastening with bobby pins. **Eg.** *"Joy say anytime papa drop her school wit her hair in cotters, errybody tease 'er all day."*

Cow Itch (kuw itch) *Noun* – **1.** a vine carrying a series of furry pods which are prickly and irritant to the skin. **2.** an itchy pod-like plant. **3.** a plant which is notorious for blistering and irritating the skin. **Eg.** *"I hear dah time when dah MLA had get Cow Itch in he jacket, people say he had run from Fort Street ta Hospital in 1.5 minutes flat."*

Cowud (kuw-udd) *Adverb* – **1.** a cowardice. **2.** a person who lacks courage in facing danger, difficulty, opposition, pain, etc; a timid or easily intimidated person. **3.** lacking courage; very fearful. **4.** Expressive of fear or timidity. **Eg.** *"Boy Chet ah real ol' cowud y'see? I hear he run 'way when burglas break in he house n' dey tek erryting."*

Cow Well (kuw well) *Noun* – **1.** a large water facility used for watering cows which may be covered on uncovered. **2.** a large water trough for cows. **Eg.** *"Daniel say one time he fall down in some horse dung n' he hadda rinse off in ah cow well."*

Crabbin' (krah-bin) *Verb* – **1.** the act of hunting for land crabs during crab season. **2.** a traditional Caymanian past time which involves a flash light, a croca sack, several large buckets and a stick. **3.** a local tradition, whereby, a group of people arrange to meet in the late evening and board a pick-up truck. From there, they will make several stops, at random, and attempt to catch around ten to fifteen crabs per stop. The last stop is usually a beach where they boil the live crabs in large pots or five gallon oil drums filled with salt water. **Eg.** *"Doon' go crabbin' with Sheila; erry time she see ah crab, she jump up n' drop da flashlight n' den da crab always get 'way."*

Crab Head (krabb hed) *Adverb* – **1.** someone who is either stubborn or difficult. **2.** a useless person. **3.** an insult targeted at a person who is being difficult. **Eg.** *"Man! Ya ol' crab head ting! You hadda go mess wit my new blouse when it nah yours, eh?"*

Crack (krah'kk) *Adjective* – **1.** crazy; stupid; insane. **2.** fool. **3.** dumb as doornails. **Eg.** *"Marshall crack yih'see? All he kin find ta talk 'bout is night fishnin' n' chasin' big woman."*

Croca Sack (cro-kah sak) *Noun* – **1.** a large potato sack. **2.** a large sack used for catching land crabs during crab season. **3.** a bag which is nearly impenetrable and has multiple uses. **Eg.** *"Ta get ready fah crab huntin', all ya need is ah flashlight, ah stick, ah croca sack, n' cupple ah buckets."*

Cry Cry Baby (kry kry bay-beh) *Adverb* – **1.** a very emotional person. **2.** one who cries excessively for no apparent reason. **3.** a softy. **4.** a pansy. **Eg.** *"Ya waugh see ah real cry cry baby? Juss take da control away from Justin when he playin' PlayStation."*

Crystal Valley (kriss-tull vah-leh) *Noun* – **1.** a housing development in West Bay which is surrounded by Mount Pleasant, Birch Tree Hill, Parkway Crescent and Papagallo Road. **2.** a popular West Bay suburb. **Eg.** *"My sista had try buy piece ah land in Crystal Valley but most ah it wah all sell out she say."*

Cun (kun) *Adverb* – **1.** can. **2.** to be able to; have the ability, power, or skill to. **3.** to know how to. **Eg.** *"Ah know ya cun fight but I gah meck sure I put some licks in ya too."*

Cuss Out (kuh'ce owt) *Verb* – **1.** to swear at or promote violence to another; verbally. **2.** to use profanity; curse; swear. **3.** to argue by tone of voice alone; minus the loud volume and profanity that is generally associated with an argument. **Eg.** *"I know if I go home widdout my homework bein' done I gah get cuss out n' I nah gah be able ta sleep ova yoh house dis weekend."*

Cut Loose (kutt loo'ce) *Verb* – **1.** to release. **2.** to give way, or give up; to deliver. **3.** to throw; let go. **Eg.** *"I memba one time when Papa Jim wah drunk, my daddy went go check im n' he cut loose one punch at im yih'see? I betcha he nah fass wit ah drunk man again afta dat"* or *"Dah time when Troy had cut loose one poomp in church, Pastor Leroy hadda bless it wit holy water before people would go back inside."*

Cutty Bush (kuh-deh bush) *Pronoun* – **1.** a former name for the area immediately behind the George Town Public Library. **2.** the former home of the Cayman Islands Boxing Association. **Eg.** *"Papa Jim say dem soljahs used ta be tick like ants rong Cutty Bush when da war wah goin' on."*

Cuzzy (cuz-eh) *Noun* – **1.** friend. **2.** brethren. **3.** cousin. **4.** a nickname for someone who is a friend or a new acquaintance. **5.** reference to someone when their name does not come to mind. **Eg.** *"Yeah cuzzy, I gah check yah back 'bout goin' Miami diss weekend."*

Cyah (k'yah) *Auxiliary Verb* – **1.** can't; cannot; can not. **2.** an expression of incapacity, inability or withholding of permission. **3.** unable to; should not; will not. **Eg.** *"It doon' madda ta me if you cyah go Miami diss weekend cuz I nah gah eeben rememba you when I up in Dolphin Mall."*

Cyar (kyarr) *Verb* – **1.** to carry. **2.** to take or support from one place to another; convey; transport:, **3.** to serve as a conduit for. **4.** to act as a bearer or conductor. **Eg.** *"Errybody kin rememba when dey use ta go supamahkit wit dey mama n' when she find all da junk dey had fill up da cart wit, she tell um muss cyar dem tings right back."*

Da (da) *Definite article* – **1.** Caymanian pronounciation of the word 'the'. **2.** used, esp. before a noun with a specifying or particularizing effect, as opposed to the indefinite or generalizing force of the indefinite article 'a' or 'an'. **Eg.** *"Da bess ting you kin do wit yoh life rite now is ta get outta my face."*

Daah (d'aahh) *Pronoun* – **1.** Caymanian pronunciation of the word 'that'. **2.** used to indicate a person, thing, idea, state, event, time, remark, etc. **Eg.** *"If I ketch you fassin' wit daah boy one more time it gah be me n' you."*

Daddy (dah-deh) *Noun* – **1.** father. **2.** one who father's a child. **3.** the male figure in a traditional family. **Eg.** *"My daddy say if I doo'n get good grades, he gah sehn me boardin' school."*

D'da-daah (duh-da-daahh) *Interjection* – **1.** whatever. **2.** something like this, or like that. **3.** this, that, and the next thing. **Eg.** *"Swee-deh, all ya gah do is turn diss ova n' d'da-daah n' it gah jess open up like nuttin'."*

D'udda Day (dih-udda day) *Adjective* – **1.** the other day. **2.** of late occurrence, appearance, or origin; lately happening, done, made, etc. **3.** years ago. **4.** a non-specific reference to the past. **Eg.** *"Gee, I cyah believe it wah juss d'udda day we wah goin' chrew Ivan n' now errybody forget it like it wah nuttin' yih'nah?"*

Dandruss (dan-d'russ) *Noun* – **1.** 'Dandruff. **2.** a seborrheic scurf that forms on the scalp and comes off in small scales. **3.** a condition in which light-coloured scales of dead skin are shed by the scalp. **Eg.** *"Any time yih gah dandruss juss go in da sea ta clear it up."*

Darkers (dar-kuz) *Noun* – **1.** really dark sunglasses. **2.** shades. **3.** eyeglasses with colored or tinted lenses that protect the eyes from the glare of sunlight. **Eg.** *"Always mek sure ta wear ya darkers when ya goin' out in bright sunlight."*

Dass (dah'ce) *Pronoun* – **1.** that's. **2.** a contraction of that is or that has. **3.** short for that had, that would, that will, that is. **Eg.** *"Dass da bess piece ah cassawa cake I ewa had in my life."*

Dat (dah't) *Pronoun* – **1.** that. **2.** used to indicate a person, thing, idea, state, event, time, remark, etc..., as pointed out or present, mentioned before, supposed to be understood, or by way of emphasis. **Eg.** *"Look ah dat eh? Dah man nah clean my car good n' talkin' bug he ready fa he money."*

Dealin' (dee-lin) *Adverb* – **1.** the third stage in the four-part structure of a relationship, which involves: *1. talkin' 2. checkin' 3. dealin' 4. goin'*. **2.** preliminary commitment to a relationship in which full monogamy is considered but not yet outlined and agreed upon. **3.** a partially-committed stage in a young relationship. **Eg.** *"Erin tell Tod she n' him nah dealin' no more cuz he love too much woman."*

Dear (dere) *Adverb* – **1.** expensive or unaffordable. **2.** a price which exceeds the ideal range of an individual. **3.** over-priced. **Eg.** *"When I wah small we used ta shop at By-Rite's cuz my mama say Merren shop wah too dear."*

Dee-Dee (dee-dee) *Noun* – **1.** waste matter discharged from the intestines through the anus; excrement. **2.** stool. **3.** number two. **4.** solid excretory product evacuated from the bowels [syn: fecal matter]. (also known as: **ca-ca**) **Eg.** *"Shawanna wah mad dah time when she had step in dee-dee wit her new shoes."*

Deh (deh) *Adverb* – **1.** there. **2.** in or at that place; opposed to 'here'. **3.** reference to either a specific or figurative location that is not in close proximity. **Eg.** *"Cranston, go out deh on da car port so see if ah drop mah swipe car from work nah?"*

Delworth's (del-wurtz) *Noun* – **1.** a popular gas station and mini mart located on the corner of Eastern Avenue and across from the Watler's Road (Dog City) area. **2.** a common hotspot for after hours snacking and loitering. **3.** the gas station across from Dixie Cemetary. **Eg.** *"I rememba when Delworth's used ta hawe da bess corn beef sangwiches in George Town."*

Dem (dehm) *Pronoun* – **1.** the objective case of 'they', used as a direct or indirect object. **2.** reference to a group of people or objects. **Eg.** *"Dem man deh always seem to be gettin' in trouble y'see."*

Dem Boys (dehm boyz) *Pronoun, Pl.* – **1.** those guys. **2.** my good friends. **3.** the fellas. **Eg.** *"Mee-mee, tell ya mama I gah be home late tonight. I goin' check dem boys cuz it Harry birtday n' we juss goin' cool out n' play some dominoes."*

Dem Old People (dem ole pee-pull) *Pronoun* – **1.** older persons or individuals who came before us. **2.** our ancestors. **3.** grandparents. **4.** all individuals over the age of 75. **5.** senior citizens. **Eg.** *"Dem old people say 'trouble doon' blow shell'. Dah why we diddn' know Ivan wah comin'."*

Dereckleh (dih-reck-leh) *Adverb* – **1.** later. **2.** the not-so-distant future. **3.** a future time to come. (also pronounced: '**ereckleh**', '**areckleh**', or '**tereckleh**' in some areas) **Eg.** *"If yah cyah doo it now juss check meh dereckleh n' I probly be ready fah yah den."*

Dew Plum (d'yoo plumb) *Noun* – **1.** a small yellowish fruit with brown spots which is sweet, yet also tartish in taste. **Eg.** *"Troy lowe ah good Dew Plum wit salt, boy."*

Didd'n Did (did'in did) *Verb* – **1.** did not do. **2.** neglected to perform a particular activity. **3.** an alibi. **Eg.** *"When da judge acks Ol' Fred if he had teef chickins outta Pastor Roy yaad, he say "no yah honour, I didd'n did it."*

Dippa (dih-pah) *Noun* – **1.** a small to medium-size bucket used to collect water from a well or cistern. **2.** a cup-like container with a long handle used for dipping liquids. **Eg.** *"One time Harry had drop da dippa in da cistern, so none ah us couldin' bade fah tree days."*

Diss (dih'ce) *Pronoun* – **1.** this; (used to indicate a person, thing, idea, state, event, time, remark, etc., as present, near, supposed to be understood, or by way of emphasis). **2.** being nearer or more immediate. **Eg.** *"Eric, come so see if diss pants kin still fit ya nah?"*

Dog City (dawg sitty) *Noun* – **1.** the Watler's Road area, first nicknamed for it's abundance of canines. **2.** the neighborhood behind Bay Town Plaza on North Church Street. **3.** a housing community located directly to the northeast of Delworth's Esso. **Eg.** *"My friend dat live dong in Dog City say she wouldn' live noway else."*

Doll Baby (dawl bay-beh) *Noun* – From West Bay **1.** any toy doll, including a *Barbie* doll. **2.** a small figure representing a baby or other human being, esp. for use as a child's toy. **Eg.** *"Mina say Melissa always use ta mess wit her doll baby when she in da bahtchroom pretendin' ta bade."*

Dong (dawng) *Adverb* – **1.** down. **2.** from higher to lower; in descending direction or order; toward, into, or in a lower position. **3.** to or in a sitting or lying position. **Eg.** *"Tell me sump'm? Why come Wess Bayas always say dey goin' up ta town and down ta Wess Bay even doh Wess Bay is da northernmost part ah Grand Cayman?"*

Donkey (dong-keh) *Noun* – **1.** a real idiot. **2.** dummy. **3.** fool. **4.** a person with little or no sense whatsoever. **Eg.** *"If I wah born ah Policeman I would arress erry donkey who try cut me off when it my turn ta cross at ah fourway stop."*

Donkey Years (dawng-key yarez) *Noun* – **1.** a very long time. **2.** years and years and years. **3.** decades ago. **Eg.** *"Pastor Ebanks bin runnin' dah church fa donkey years now."*

Doon' (doo'n) *Verb* – **1.** contraction of *do not*. **2.** be careful. *Noun* – **3.** a statement of what should not be done. **Eg.** *"Pee-Wee! Doon' go in my room when I nah deh man! I gah private stuff in deh yih'nah?"*

Draws (drawz) *Noun* – **1.** one's underwear; briefs or panties **2.** any undergarment. **3.** bloomers. **Eg.** *"Mummy, yestaday Lionel tell Randel he mama wear croca sack draws n' Randel tek one big rock n' pelt im right in he head yih'nah."*

Druggy (druh-geh) *Noun* – **1.** one who takes or is addicted to drugs. **2.** any individual who is known to consume marijuana, cocaine, heroin, or any other narcotic on a regular basis. **3.** a drug addict. **4.** one who loves drugs more than life itself. **Eg.** *"Mahma, one druggy juss walk chrew ouwah yard and teef Daddy boxers off da clothesline."*

Duppy (duh-peh) *Imaginary Noun* – **1.** a ghost, shadow or spirit of a dead person. **2.** a disembodied spirit imagined, usually as a vague, shadowy or evanescent form, as wandering among or haunting living persons. **3.** a reason to be afraid while walking at night. **Eg.** *"I hate walkin' chrew town when it dark cuz I 'fraid duppy gah ketch me."*

Duss Out (duss owt) *Verb* – **1.** to leave in a great haste. **2.** to stir up dust by kicking, scraping or rotating car tires at a high velocity. **3.** gone with the wind. **Eg.** *"If yah waugh see people duss out jess acks fah help wit cleanin' up afta ah big party."*

Dusta (dus-tah) *Noun* – **1.** a woman's lightweight sleeping garment. **2.** a thin, robe-like garment which covers a woman's bed clothes; including pajamas and lingerie. **Eg.** *"Granny always used ta hawe on her dusta from 6:00 in da evenin' even doh she diddn' go bed 'til 8:00."*

Dyappah (die-yap-ah) *Noun* – **1.** diaper. **2.** a piece of cloth or other absorbent material folded and worn as underpants by a baby not yet toilet-trained. **3.** a linen or cotton fabric with a woven pattern of small, constantly repeated figures, as diamonds. **Eg.** *"I hate changin' my lil' sista diyappah. She always hawe dee-dee all owa da place n' she be pee-pee'in' while ya tryin' change 'er."*

Dyke Road (dyke rode) *Noun* – **1.** one in a series of roads which were carved into the swamps throughout the Islands to create a passage for the *'fogger'* - a truck armed with chemicals for controlling mosquitos. **2.** a side road made of white marl (usually through a swamp) which has not been authorized for public use. **Eg.** *"I feel sorry fa anybody who get ketch down in dem dike roads wit no flash light cuz some ah dem be full ah duppies."*

Dd

Ear Hole (air hoal) *Noun* – **1.** the entrance to one's ear. **2.** a passage between the inner ear and outer ear. **3.** part of the instrument used for receiving sound, which is processed by the brain. **Eg.** *"Lissin' yah man. If ya cyah hear wah I sayin', clean yah ear hole next time n' stop acksin' so much questions."*

East (eace) *Adverb* – **1.** the eastern districts, including; Bodden Town, Breakers, East End and North Side. **2.** a cardinal point of the compass, 90-degrees to the right of north. **3.** the longitude of the area from which the sun rises. **Eg.** *"Anytime I go East I always feel like I in ah diffrunt country cuz it so peaceful."*

East End (eece-tend) *Noun* – **1.** the second largest district on Grand Cayman with an area of approximately 20.9 square miles and a population of 1,064 people (1989 census). **2.** the area of which has been rumored to belong to William Foster in 1741 during a land grant of 100 plus acres. Foster supposedly lived in this area with his servants and slaves for a time, but migrated later to Bodden Town and then Cayman Brac (1833). **3.** the easternmost district on Grand Cayman. **4.** the place where East Enders live. **5.** a good place for spear fishin', surfin' and reef divin'. **Eg.** *"Dem East End boys always lowe brag about how good dey kin' fishin' betta dan Wess Bayas."*

Eat Out (eet owtt) *Verb* – **1.** to devour every morsel in sight. **2.** to swallow or eat up hungrily, voraciously, or ravenously. **3.** to consume destructively, recklessly, or wantonly. **Eg.** *"If I eva ketch whoeva eat out my Funyuns it gah be pure licks fah da person."*

Edieyut (eed'yutt) *Noun* – **1.** an idiot. **2.** anyone who lacks common knowledge or common sense. **3.** a fool. **Eg.** *"Lissin' ta me? You tink I ah edieyut ah wah? I know it nah no such ting as fortylebbenteen, but it song like ah big numba so I like it"* or; *Margaret!? I tell you ta keep da birtday party small n' you gone n' invite fortylebbenteen people ta come mash up my house?*

Eech (ee'ch) *Adjective* – **1.** to itch. **2.** to have or feel a peculiar tingling or uneasy irritation of the skin that causes a desire to scratch the part affected. **Eg.** *"Sometimes I gah sleep wit no sheet cuz it be eechin' me man."*

Eeble (ee-bull) *Adjective* – **1.** a combination of the words *even* and *able*, meaning; just. **2.** having the ability to perform. **3.** capable without obstruction or hesitation. **Eg.** *"You couldn' eeble hurt ah fly if you tried."*

Eed'yut (ee-d'yutt) *Noun* – **1.** a complete and total idiot. **2.** an utterly foolish or senseless person. **3.** a person so mentally deficient as to be incapable of ordinary reasoning. **4.** an uneducated or ignorant person. **Eg.** *"You's ah real eed'yut fa lennin' Pursley yoh bicycle again."*

Eeease (eeee'zzz) *Interjection* – **1.** cool. **2.** excellent; first rate. **3.** a general response to a favourable statement. **4.** acceptable; satisfactory. **Eg.** *"Bobby: Cuz, check out diss new Playstation game my friend bring me from Japan nah? O'neil: Eeeaase... it look criss still. Lemme play first nah?"*

Een (een) *Preposition* – Primarily from East End; **1.** in. **2.** on the inside; within. **3.** used to indicate inclusion within something abstract or immaterial. **Eg.** *"Harry it come een like Josie Lee cyah cook fish or sump'm cuz she always be bunnin' up errying I bring home when I go fishnin'."*

Either or Either (ee-thur er eye-thur) *Adjective* – **1.** either way. **2.** anyway. **3.** however. **4.** whatever. **5.** don't care. **6.** a way of showing indecisiveness or lack of concern or commitment. **Eg.** *"Either or either way I still know you gah go behind my back n' doo foolishniss."*

Ee

Elizabethan (ee-liz-uh-bee-tun) *Noun* – **1.** Elizabethan Square. **2.** one of the most active business complexes in George Town. **3.** the current location of the Monetary Authority Building, Cayman Travel Services and FedEx. **Eg.** *"Me n' my gyalfriend use ta hawe lunch around da fountain at Elizabethan erry day."*

Ereckleh (eh-reck-leh) *Adverb* – **1.** later. **2.** the not-so-distant future. **3.** a future time to come. (also pronounced: 'areckleh', 'dereckleh', or 'tereckleh' in some areas) **Eg.** *"check meh ereckleh, n' I gah see wah we kin doo."* or; *Mama, Miss Anne say she gah check ya ereckleh cuz she goin' church t'night n' it nah gah be ova til late."*

Errybody (err-eh baw-deh) *Pronoun* – **1.** everybody. **2.** every person. **3.** everyone. **4.** all persons involved. **5.** the whole crew. **Eg.** *"It kinda funny how ya cyah invite errybody ta ya weddin but dey still come ta ya funeral."* or; *'Boy Cresley beach party wah nice nah? Errybody n' dey mama wah deh whinin' up n' bouncin' rong like dey had jess win da lottery."*

Erryting (err-eh ting) *Pronoun* – **1.** every thing. **2.** every aspect or particular of an aggregate or total; all. **3.** something extremely important: *it means erryting to me.* **Eg.** *"When playin' marbles we use ta call erryting on da next man taw n' he could'n say nuttin'."*

Erryway (err-eh way) *Pronoun* – **1.** every where. **2.** in every place or part; in all places. **3.** all over. **4.** vast coverage. **Eg.** *"Erryway ya go it seem like yih kin' buy phone cards or cigarettes easier dun yih kin buy food."*

Ever Glow (ev-ah glo) *Pronoun* – **1.** the trade name of a former drive-in movie theatre located in Pease Bay during the 1970s and 80s. **2.** one of the most popular hotspots during the late 1970s and early 1980s. **3.** an outdoor motion picture theatre and refreshment stand designed to accommodate patrons in their automobiles. **Eg.** *"I always use'ta love watchin' dem ol' black n' white kung fu movies at Ever Glow drive-in. Da ones wit Bruce Lee wah da bess."*

Facety (fay'ce-teh) *Adjective* – **1.** full of audacity. **2.** bold. **3.** not hesitating to break the rules of propriety; forward; impudent. **4.** enterprising. **5.** assuming; rude; sassy; immodest. **6.** smart-alecky. **Eg.** *"Dat facety gyal gah soon get ah sahpapah if she doon' hush up."*

Fah (fuh) *Preposition* – **1.** for. **2.** with the object or purpose of. **3.** intended to belong to, or be used in connection with. **Eg.** *"I hate when dem ol' people acks 'who you fah?' n' dey neva know who ya mama n' daddy is when ya tell um."*

Farm Soldier (fahrm sol-jah) *Noun* – **1.** a position held by Caymanian O'chester "Pad'sin" Patterson during World War II. **2.** the words which were emblazoned on the back of Ochester Patterson's army jacket, which he wore with pride, and defended jealously. **Eg.** *"I like how Luigi re-make dem Farm Soldier t-shirts yih'see. Now dass some real Caymanian stuff man."*

Fass (fahce) *Verb* – **1.** fast. **2.** moving or able to move, operate, function, or take effect quickly; quick; swift; rapid. *Adverb* – **3.** mischievous and bothersome. **4.** troublesome. **Eg.** *"Randy juss lowe ta fass wit da gyals on da bus, but one time Leanne fix he bizness fa him."*

Fass-eh (fah'ce-ih) *Pronoun* – **1.** one who interferes with the property or affairs of others. **2.** a mischiefmaker. **3.** a browser. **4.** a busybody. **Eg.** *"You ol' fass-eh. Why u hadda go trubble my 'Days of Our Lives fah?"*

Fassniss (fah'ce-niss) *Adjective* – **1.** mischievousness. **2.** child-like playfulness. **Eg.** *"I dunno why you hadda mess wit my car wit yah fassniss n' now it nah workin'."*

Fass Hand (fahce han) *Adverb* – **1.** having the propensity to handle the property of others without permission. **2.** compelled to steal. **3.** thieving. **4.** unable to resist the temptation to mis-handle the property of others. **Eg.** *"Dah ol' fass hand ting ah Corbert always be messin' wit my stuff."*

Feel Up (feele-upp) *Verb* – **1.** to touch or fondle something inappropriately. **2.** to handle an object in an unbecoming manner. **3.** to examine extensively by touching. **Eg.** *"It hard to get wah ya waugh sometimes, cuz even when ya go supamahkit all da fruits be all feel up."*

Feva Grass (fee-vuh grah'ce) *Noun* – From Old People Times; **1.** an old wives remedy for most types of fever. **2.** a green grass found in most overgrown areas which has herbal qualities and is used to treat colds and fever. **3.** a 'bush med'sin'; drunk as a tea. **Eg.** *"Even if yih nah gah no med'sin yih kin always go pick some feva grass."*

Fiancheh (fee-yahn-chehh) *Noun* – **1.** one's fiance'. **2.** a man or woman who is engaged to be married; a man to whom a woman is engaged. **3.** one's future husband or wife. **Eg.** *"I dunno why Gilbert still tellin' people det Detty he fiancheh when he still be foolin' rong wit Paulette."*

Fingas (fee'ng-ahz) *Noun, Pl.* – **1.** a nickname for Caymanian dumplings. **2.** the five digits of the hand. **Eg.** *"I love when babies hold onto my hand wit dey lil' fingas."*

File Paypah (fyle pay-puh) *Noun* – **1.** foil paper; a thin, metal wrapping made of foil, for the purpose of protecting food from bacteria, insects, dust and mould. **2.** an essential cooking item. **Eg.** *"Anytime I see my nevyew puttin' file paypah on he teet I jess gah shake my head cuz he look like dah guy "Jaws" from James Bond."*

Fire Box (fye-ah bawkz) *Noun* – From Old People Times; **1.** a small wooden box filled with sand and candle-wood, which was burned to produce light at night. **2.** an early alternative to lamps and lanterns. **3.** a traditional Cayman light source. **Eg.** *"Dey say one time it wah easy ta get stuff ta put in ya fire box but yah cyah hardly do dat no more."*

Ff

Fishnin' (fish-nin) *Verb* – **1.** fishing. **2.** the act of catching fish. **3.** to fish for food on water using a boat, or on land, via ironshore. **4.** the technique, occupation, or diversion of catching fish. **Eg.** *"My unka Harold cun fishnin' betta dun mos' people in East End."*

Fish Pot (fish pawt) *Noun* – **1.** a 'fish trap', which is made from sticks and chicken wire, and placed in shallow waters to collect fish, lobsters, and conch. **2.** a large box, whose frame can be made from lightweight timber, and outlined in chicken wire; used for capturing fish near to shore or in shallow waters. **3.** a great way to catch fish without using bait. **Eg.** *"Sometimes ya gah curry up yah fish pot or else somebody gah steal it when ya nah deh."*

Fish Tea (fih-she tee) *Noun* – **1.** a traditional Caymanian soup made primarily from small fish such as grunts, squabs (parrot fish), butterfish, doctor fish, etc. mixed with breadkind, salt, pepper, onions and other seasonings. **2.** a standard menu item at any Caribbean restaurant in Cayman. **Eg.** *"Boy diss wah ya call some good ol' fish tea!"*

Fix Wheel Bicycle (fickz weel by-sick'l) *Noun* – **1.** a constricted alteration of one's bicycle crank shaft to increase speed. **2.** a bicycle that is really difficult to stop. **Eg.** *"Yestaday when we wah jumpin' in da sea up by Smit Barcadere somebody teef Eldon fix wheel bicycle."*

Fiyah Antses (f'eye-yah ahntz-iz) *Noun, Pl.* – **1.** large stinging ants. **2.** an army of large black or red ants which are notorious for painful bites. **3.** a species of the red ant. **4.** biting ants. **Eg.** *"Anytime ya go rake da yaad, yih cyah help but get bite up by fiyah antses."*

Flawesome (flaugh-sum) *Slang* – **1.** flawlessly awesome. **2.** a combination of the words *"flawless"* and *"awesome"*. **3.** something that is extremely excellent. **4.** an expression to use when there is no other word to describe something great. **Eg.** *"I used to be flawesome at doin' flips offa da iron shore when I wah small."*

Fling (fleengh) *Verb* – **1.** to throw, cast, or hurl with force or violence. **2.** to move an object from one space to another by throwing. **3.** to transport. **Eg.** *"Mama, kin u come fling me ta da movies, please?"*

Flitters (flih-duz) *Noun, Pl.* – **1.** traditional Caymaian buns, having a yellowish-brown colour and made of flour, salt, butter, baking powder, and having a solid crust on the outside and a soft, sweet inside. **2.** one of the most popular side dishes for any meal, especially fried fish. **Eg.** *"Gee-doh! Yoh Daddy kin mek frittas good yih'see? Axe im if I kin cyar some ah deez home nah?"*

Flood Out (fludd owt) *Noun* – **1.** to overcome with water or other substance. **2.** overflowing with water. *Adverb* – **3.** the state of most houses following Hurricane Ivan. **Eg.** *"In 1988, I went Miami fa ah week n' when I come back Gilbert had my house all flood out."*

Flowa Nose (fluh-wah nohz) *Noun* – **1.** an odd-shaped pair of nostrils that are usually flared and twisted or irregular. **2.** a funny looking nose. **Eg.** *"Oh my Gosh, Hilary, looka Lucy-Ann boyfriend. Way he goin' wit dah flowa nose, man?"*

Flusstrated (fluh'ce-tray-did) *Adjective* – **1.** flustered and frustrated. **2.** disappointed; thwarted. **3.** thrown into a state of agitated confusion. **Eg.** *"Maannn! Lee me alone nah? You juss gets me so flusstrated sometimes I juss waugh grab ya n' shake ya ta pieces."*

Folla Fashion (foh-lah fash-un) *Adjective* – **1.** inclined to follow others; a follower. **2.** a human sheep. **3.** one who lacks individuality or originality. **4.** void of originalality. **Eg.** *"Ya too folla fashion man. Erryting I do, you ga do it too."*

Fooleh (foo-leh) *Noun* – **1.** a silly or stupid person; one who lacks judgement or sense. **2.** someone who loves to tease others. **3.** a dummy. **4.** an idiot. **Eg.** *"You ol' fooleh, you cyah hear I doon' like eggs wit pancakes ah wah?"*

Fool-Fool (fool-fool) *Noun* – **1.** crazy. **2.** a nutcase. **3.** a complete idiot. **4.** a rampaging maniac. **5.** a mentally deranged person; demented; insane. **Eg.** *"Do not mess wit Brenard when he eatin' he dumplins! He fool-fool yih'nah."*

Fooshniss (foo-sh-niss) *Noun* – **1.** foolishness. **2.** resulting from or showing a lack of sense; ill-considered; unwise. **3.** lacking forethought or caution. **4.** trifling, insignificant, or paltry. **Eg.** *"I hadda walk outta dah movie lass night, cuz it wah nuttin' but fooshniss man."*

Football (foot-bawl) *Noun* – **1.** the world's most popular sport. **2.** the Cayman Islands' national sport. **3.** any of various games played with a ball in which two teams try to kick the ball across a field and into each other's goal. **Eg.** *"Anytime I hear people callin' football 'soccer', it mek meh giddy cuz I doon' know who made up dah name."*

Formin' (faw'r-min) *Verb* – **1.** pretending. **2.** acting. **3.** demonstrating; giving a false appearance. **Eg.** *"Anytime my mama used ta ketch me formin' like I wah sleepin' she used ta slap me in my head."*

Forrid (faw-rid) *Noun* – **1.** the human forehead. **2.** the part of the face above the eyebrows; brow. **3.** the fore or front part of anything. **Eg.** *"Lucas get tease in class all da time cuz he gah one piece ah forrid on im y'see?"*

Fortylebbenteen (for-deh-leb-in-tene) *Adjective* – **1.** any high number that is seemingly impossible to count. **2.** a lot. **3.** an unbelievable amount. **Eg.** *"I hear say dey gah 'bout fortylebbenteen chickens up by Franklin Farm."*

Fritters (frih-duz) *Noun, Pl.* – **1.** traditional Caymanian buns, having a yellowish-brown colour, and made of flour, salt, butter, baking powder, and having a solid crust on the outside and a soft, sweet inside. **2.** one of the most popular side dishes for any meal, especially fried fish. **3.** a small yellow bun. (also called: **Flitters**) **Eg.** *"Way Bobby gone? Tell im bring back some ah dem flitters he teef from out da kitchen or else he gah hawe deal wit me."*

Full Up (full upp) *Verb, trans.* – **1.** filled; stuffed; packed. **2.** to lack availability within a place or thing. **3.** to fill with people or objects or substance. **4.** to exceed capacity. **Eg.** *"Anytime I go Fosta's on Satdeh mornin' it always be full-up wit people, so I jess go get my hair done n' come back."*

Furd (fird) *Adverb* – **1.** far. **2.** at or to a great distance; a long way off; at or to a remote point. **3.** far far away. **4.** too far to be measured. **Eg.** *"I had ta get a car because five miles is too furd for me ta walk ta work erry mornin'."*

Ff

Gah (g'ah) *Verb* – **1.** to have. **2.** going to. **3.** have to. **4.** to cause to, as by command or invitation. **5.** to show or exhibit in action or words. **Eg.** *"If you doon' do it, I gah have ta do it."*

Galavant (gal-a-vahnt) *Verb* – **1.** to roam about in search of pleasure or amusement. **2.** to walk around endlessly for no apparent reason. **3.** to prance around town sporting new clothes, hoping that others will see. **Eg.** *"If ya see Paul-O galavantin' all day, he mad up 'bout sump'm."*

Galleon (gyal-yun) *Noun* – **1.** Galleon Beach. **2.** the former Galleon Beach Hotel. **3.** one of the first luxury hotels on Grand Cayman. **4.** the area between the Ritz-Carlton Hotel and the Governor's House. **Eg.** *"My mama use ta work down by Galleon Beach Hotel in da 60's."*

Gapseed (gyap-seed) *Noun* – **1.** the verbal passage of fresh information. **2.** chatter; hearsay; news. *Verb* – **3.** to engage in idle talk or rumor, esp. about the personal or private affairs of others. **4.** rumor mongering. **Eg.** *"Erry election time all kinda gapseed be spreadin' bout dem MLA's."*

Gauldin' (gawl-din) *Noun* – **1.** a tall, skinny person with bird-like legs. **2.** any of numerous long-legged, long-necked, usually long-billed birds of the family *Ardeidae*. **Eg.** *"Fredrick look like one ol' long neck gauldin' y'see?"*

Guava (g'augh-wah) *Noun* – **1.** a small yellowish fruit, filled with seeds and a pasty inside. **2.** a fruit, used for making jam, jelly, etc. **3.** a large lump on one's head after physical contact with a blunt object. **Eg.** *"My tweedums, lil' Joseph juss fall down n' get ah lil' guava on he head."*

Gauwa Dosey (gaw-ah doh-seh) *Noun* – **1.** a thick, solid, jelly-like jam which has origins in Cuba, but has become known as '*sweet meat*' throughout the Cayman Islands. **2.** a thick jam-like treat, similar to a sweet heavy cake, made entirely from guava. **Eg.** *"Gimme ah good slice ah gauwa dosey any day n' I'll love you fa life."*

Gee (jee) *Interjection* – **1.** wow. **2.** an exclamation of extreme surprise. **3.** holy mackerel. **4.** oh my gosh! **5.** short for '*geezumpiece*'. **Eg.** *"Gee! You see how furd he kin jump man?"*

Geezum (jee-z'um) *Interjection* – **1.** an expression of excitement and disbelief. **2.** oh goodness. **3.** really? **4.** I can't believe it. **5.** oh-my-gosh. **6.** one's first reaction to a major accident or natural disaster. (used interchangeably with: **Geezumpiece**) **Eg.** *"Geezumpiece! I didd'n tink Iwan woulda mash up da place like diss!"*

George Town (jorge town) *Noun* – **1.** the capital district of the Cayman Islands. **2.** one of the world's leading financial centers. **3.** the second capital district of the Cayman Islands (Bodden Town was first). **Eg.** *"My mail keep gettin' sent ta Guyana and Washington sometimes, cuz dey also have ah George Town."*

George Town Barcadere (jawr'j taown bar-kuh-dehr) *Noun* – **1.** a former name for the embankment at the very end of North Sound Road which opens up to the North Sound. **2.** a boat dock and marina near the CUC power plant. **Eg.** *"I hear Curry used ta go swimmin' by George Town Barcadere till people tell im it wah full ah jellyfish."*

Gi (g'ee) *Verb* – **1.** to give. **2.** to present voluntarily and without expecting compensation; bestow. **3.** to hand to someone. **4.** to furnish, provide, or proffer. **Eg.** *"When I finish wit dis movie I gah gi it ta you, but you bedda cyar it bak Blockbusta when ya finish."*

Giddy-Giddy (gih-deh gih-deh) *Adverb* – **1.** extremely giddy. **2.** affected with vertigo; dizzy. **3.** attended with or causing dizziness. *Noun* – **4.** lightheaded, vertiginous. **Eg.** *"Sometimes when I sleep too much I feel kinda giddy-giddy when I stand up so I juss lay back down n' sleep again."*

Giddy Head (gih-deh hed) *Adjective* – **1.** indecisive and incompetent. **2.** unable to make up one's mind or make constructive decisions. **3.** free-spirited. **Eg.** *"Why you don't try stop foolin' rong wit dem giddy head gyals n' fine ah half-decent woman ta settle down wit?"*

Gig (gihg) *Noun* – **1.** a small wooden toy, often inversely conical, with a point on which it is made to spin. **2.** a store-bought or handmade 'top'. **3.** a favourite pastime among Caymanian boys up until the late 1980's. **Eg.** *"Ian kin spin gig good boy. I see im split Ed gig in two lass week."*

Goggle Eye (gaw-gul eye) *Noun* – **1.** a person with enormous eyes. **2.** a greedy person. **3.** a very nosey person. **4.** a small saltwater fish also known as a *frisky gog* or *bigeye scad*. **Eg.** *"Look ah dah ol' goggle eye ting droolin' ohwah erryting he see nah?"*

Goin' (goh-yin) *Verb* – **1.** the final stage in the four-part structure of a relationship, which involves: *1. talkin' 2. checkin' 3. dealin' 4. goin'*. **2.** commited to a serious relationship. **3.** embarking on a long-term relationship. **4.** having a boyfriend or gyalfriend. **Eg.** *"If you don't stop chattin' up Christina me n' you nah goin' no more."*

Goin' Off (goh-yin awf) *Adverb* – **1.** going crazy. **2.** losing one's sanity. **3.** getting really angry. **4.** losing control. **5.** becoming entempered. **Eg.** *"David be goin' off sometimes at work cuz dem customers be gettin' on he nerves."*

Goin' Out Clothes (goh-in owt kloh'ze) *Noun* – **1.** one's dress clothes. **2.** good clothes. **3.** the best clothes in one's closet. **4.** smart casual or semi-formal attire. **Eg.** *"Richard, you diddn' have ta wear ya goin' out clothes ta come ova my house fa ah babbecue."*

Gone Clear (gawn kleer) *Adverb* – **1.** free and clear. **2.** in the clear. **3.** successful. **Eg.** *"Yeah, ya gone clear now doh! I know you had really waugh dah job and ya get it too!"*

Goodnight! (gud-nyte) *Interjection* – **1.** an exclamatory expression of excitement or amazement. **2.** watch out. **3.** a warning of something to come. **Eg.** *"Goodnight! I know he mussa tear up he pants when he fall off dah bicycle."*

Gg

Gowament (gow-ah-mehnt) *Noun* – **1.** the government. **2.** the form or system of rule by which a country is governed. **3.** the Cabinet, all Elected Members, departments, statutory authorities, etc... **Eg.** *"I hear one man det used ta wuk fa gowament in India gettin' paid $1 ah day fa he pension. I glad we nah gah deal wit daah."*

Granny (grah-neh) *Noun* – **1.** a grandmother. **2.** an elderly woman. **3.** a fussy individual who has very little or no teeth. **4.** a woman, whose children have children of their own. **Eg.** *"Granny used ta mix up all kinda bush med'sin ta correck my liss tongue, but it diddn' work."*

Granny Dress (grah-neh dreh'ce) *Noun* – **1.** a large ugly dress. **2.** any ill-fitting dress which is either old or unfashionable. **Eg.** *"Mummy, how you expeck me ta wear dah ol' granny dress ta my prom?"*

Granfadda (gran-fah-dah) *Noun* – **1.** the father of one's father or mother. **2.** a forefather. **3.** an old man who smells like vwick's sahwe (vick's rub), chews tobacco, and wears nothing but khaki pants and marina's. **Eg.** *"My granfadda wuz ah really popula man fah some reason. I tink it muss be cuz he wah up in gowament."*

Granfadda Pants (gran-fah-dah pahnt'z) *Noun* – **1.** any tight, unfashionable pants, having no pleats, stitching, or bagginess whatsoever. **2.** really ugly pants. **Eg.** *"Erry time Andrew mama fa'get ta wash he always come school wit deez granfadda pants."*

Grass Piece (grah'ce pee'ce) *Noun* – **1.** an extensive, level or somewhat undulating, mostly treeless tract of land on which cows and horses are free to graze. **2.** piece of bush land for feedin' cows. **3.** a cow pasture. **Eg.** *"Wheneva ya walk chrew Mista Powell grasspiece yau bet'nah be wearin' red cuz dah bull gah run ya ova wit dem horns."*

Graveyard Fruit (gray'vh yahrd froot) *Noun* – **1.** *Morinda citrifolia*, Noni; a shrub or small tree in the family *Rubiaceae*. **2.** a local reference to the *Noni* fruit; a greenish-yellow fruit which is prickly on the outside, filled with seeds (similar to a sour sop), and commonly found in graveyards throughout the Islands. **Eg.** *"Some say ya mussn' eat wah dey call graveyard fruit, but I hear it good fa yah."*

Ground Provisions (graown pruh-vizgh-unz) *Noun, Pl.* – **1.** any vegetables or other produce which has been grown or cultivated in the earth. **2.** roots and other vegetables grown underground such as: yam, cassava, lettuce and cabbage. **Eg.** *"I dunno wah I would do if I diddn' have no ground provisions ta go wit my Fry Snappa."*

Guinep (gih-nip) *Noun* – **1.** *Melicoccus Bijugatus;* a round tropical fruit bearing a large seed and a sweet juicy translucent pulp; encased in a leathery shell. **2.** one of Cayman's favourite seasonal fruits. **3.** a fruit which varies in taste due to the quality of the soil in which the tree is planted. **Eg.** *"All ya gah do is bring one bag ah guineps ta work n' people gah love ya fah life."*

Gun Bay (guhn bay) *Noun* – **1.** a community in the district of *East End*. **2.** the area between the town of *East End* and the area known as *Colliers*. **Eg.** *"No, fool-eh, I nah from East End, I from Gun Bay."*

Gun Square (gun sk'ware) *Noun* – **1.** a point of defence in the District of Bodden Town in the early days of settlement; identified by two of the original cannons pointing in the ground. **2.** a battery which was very important to Bodden Town as it overlooked the district's principal channels of the day. **Eg.** *"I hear dey ketch one man walkin' rong drunk up by Gun Square. Dey say he wah only wearin' he brief n' nuttin' else."*

Gyahbbage (gyah-bidge) *Noun* – **1.** garbage. **2.** a collection of solid or liquid waste. **3.** discarded animal or vegetable matter, as from a kitchen; refuse. **4.** any matter that is no longer wanted or needed; trash. **Eg.** *"Moo frum rong yah wit dah piece ah gyahbbage man."*

Gyal (g'yull) *Noun* – **1.** any person belonging to the female gender. **2.** a woman or girl. **3.** a female child, from birth to full growth. **4.** a young, immature woman; a young unmarried female. **Eg.** *"Aye you gyal, you waugh come wit me ta Kimmin' Brike fa da weekend ah wah?"*

Gye'n (gye'nh) *Adjective* – **1.** going. **2.** leaving or departing. **3.** the process of moving from one position to the other. (see also: **gine**) **Eg.** *"Morris, I hear say you gye'n Miami diss weekend."*

Had Went (hahd went) *Verb* – **1.** past tense of the word 'go'. **2.** went. **3.** to have gone before. **Eg.** *"Dah time when me n' Wilfurd had went Miami Carnival, we come back wit nuff gyal phone numbas."*

Hahwe (ha'hwe) *Verb* – **1.** *have*; to possess; own; hold for use; contain. **2.** to hold, get, receive, or take. **3.** to experience. **Eg.** *"I doon' know why, but somehow you juss always hawe ta touch my stuff."*

Harden (hard-inn) *Adverb* – **1.** hard of hearing. **2.** having reduced or deficient hearing ability. **3.** unwilling or unable to learn. **4.** stubborn and ignorant. **5.** fixed or set in purpose or opinion. **Eg.** *"Boy you harden yih'see! Erry time I tell you ta leawe my iPod alone, you keep fassin' wid it like it yours."*

Haven (hay-vin) *Noun* – **1.** the first feature length film to be written and directed by Frank E. Flowers Jr. **2.** the first movie filmed entirely in the Cayman Islands. **3.** an independent film featuring nuff nuff Caymanians as extras. **Eg.** *"Frank-eh really did ah good job on Haven, still."*

Hawk Up (hawk ap) *Verb* – **1.** to make an effort to raise phlegm from the throat. **2.** to bring up cold. **3.** a noisy effort to clear the throat. **Eg.** *"One time when I wah wukkin' supamahkit, Troy had hawk up cold n' spit it on da ceilin."*

Heavy Foot (heh-vih foot) *Noun* – **1.** the inability to control one's foot or feet, properly. **2.** having an affinity for speed. **Eg.** *"Daddy always be screamin' at Dara, cuz she gah one heavy foot n' he tell her she nah gah pass her driver's licence if she doon' slow down."*

Hedgehog (hay'dj hawg) *Noun* – **1.** a *'Balloonfish'* or *'Globefish'* (*Diodon holocanthus*); a species of *'Pufferfish'*, having very long spines on its head and body, while appearing to have dusky bands of colour over its body. **2.** a fish which has the ability to suck in large amounts of water until it is the size of a football. **3.** a bug-eyed fish with crusty lips, large spikes and a flat head. **Eg.** *"Daddy, kin people eat Hedgehog?; or dey juss da kine a fish yah ketch and fling back in da sea?"*

Hell (hehl) *Noun* – **1.** an area of the district of West Bay which features a unique, complex pattern of pinnacles and miniature ridges intricately sculptured into jagged, sharp-edged masses which are quite hard but at the same time brittle. The formation is said to be about 2 million years old and its gray/blackened colour is due to the weather and algae activity. **2.** the area of West Bay which earned its name after a time when Commissioner Cardinall and a friend were out shooting. After the friend missed a bird, he uttered the words "Oh Hell", which, among other things, led the commissioner to name the place 'Hell'. **3.** an area of the district of West Bay which was formerly known as 'fountain'. **4.** the area comprising of the Hell Gas Station, the Hell Post Office, and the nightclub *Inferno*. **Eg.** *"I dunno how come errybody be teckin' one whole pile ah pitchas ah Hell fah."*

He Tree (hee tree) *Noun* – **1.** any species of fruit bearing tree which is infertile or barren. **2.** a 'male tree'. **3.** a fruit tree which is unable to bear viable fruit, although some tend to blossom and produce fruit which are empty or inedible inside. **Eg.** *"I hate when guinep season come. Da only tree close ta my house is ah He Tree n' I nah gah no way ta go lookin' fa ah next one."*

Hiccatee (hih-k-ah-tee) *Noun* – **1.** (also called: **Higgity**) a fresh water *terrapin*. **2.** one of Cayman's rare freshwater turtles, which dwells primarly in ponds and swamps throughout the Islands. **3.** an ugly little snapping turtle. **4.** a species of reptile of the order *Testudines*, of which most of its body is shielded by a special bony or cartilagenous shell developed from its ribs. **Eg.** *"Watch out! Yih gah run ova dah lil' baby hiccatee!"*

Hh

Hickly Pickly (hik-leh pik-leh) *Adverb* – **1.** in a state of disorder or disarray. **2.** chaotic. **3.** messy and disorganized. **4.** unbelievably messy. (also: **hicklety-pickle**) **Eg.** *"Sandra! How you expect Jodie Ann to come sleep ova when you gah yoh room so hickly pickly?"*

High Up (hye upp) *Adjective* – **1.** in a euphoric state as a result of inducing alcohol, drugs, etc. **2.** high on drugs. **Eg.** *"Boy, you shoulda see how you had look diss mornin' when you wake up. You wah all high up so I hadda leave ya right deh so ya could ress up lil' bit."*

High Tide (hye tyde) *Adjective* – **1.** shrunken or shortened; as in pants which are unable to reach one's shoes. **2.** old-fashioned clothing. **Eg.** *"I wouldn' be caught dead or alive wit dem ol' high tide pants on."*

Hidda (hih-duh) *Noun* – **1.** a junkie or drug addict. **2.** one who is addicted to narcotics. **3.** a cokehead. (see also: **druggy** or **drughead**) **Eg.** *"You had look like ah hidda dah time when you came school all drug up wit cold medicine."*

Hoggish (hawg-ish) *Adverb* – **1.** coarsely self-indulgent or gluttonous. **2.** selfish. **3.** befitting a hog. **4.** unable to control one's temptation to eat excessively. **Eg.** *"Burman n' Nicole got ah divorce cuz erry time they went out he went on too hoggish."*

Hog Plum (hawg pluhm) *Noun* – **1.** *Spondias mombin*; a fruit which has leathery skin and a thin layer of pulp. The pulp is either eaten fresh or made into juice, concentrate, jellies and sherbets. (also called: *Yellow Mombin, Spanish Plum, Gully Plum, Ashanti Plum, True Yellow Mombin, Golden Apple,* or *Java Plum*) **Eg.** *"Bobo, hook meh up wit one ah dem hog plums nah? I nah eat nuttin' all day."*

Hog Sty Bay (hawg stye bay) *Noun* – **1.** a large bay, (leading into the George Town area) which was originally titled "*Ye Hoggstyes*" in the 1700s, for its modest trade in yams, limes, fowls and hoggs. **2.** the primary location for the annual Schooner Regatta during the early 20th Century. **3.** the body of water in which cruise ships are parked during tourist visits. **Eg.** *"Wheneva ya see Hog Sty Bay full ah cruise ships, yih know dem tourist shops gah mek money, n' tourisses gah be walkin' up in down blockin' traffic."*

Holla (haw-lah) *Verb* – **1.** to scream or shout loudly. **2.** a very loud utterance. **3.** to call out to someone from a great distance. **Eg.** *"If somebody axe you fah ah dolla, tell um muss go down in da Sound n' holla."*

Hongry (hawng-greh) *Adverb* – **1.** hungry. **2.** having a desire, craving, or need for food: feeling hunger. **3.** strongly or eagerly desirous. **4.** marked by a scarcity of food. **Eg.** *"Boy try so go feed dah ol' hongry belly dog."*

Horse Laugh (hawr'se lahf) *Noun* – **1.** an uncontrollable outburst of laughter. **2.** rough and noisy, jolly or rowdy, clamorous, unrestrained laughter. **Eg.** *"Dah time when Samuel had run ta he car in da rain n' slip down in one big puddle ah mud, errybody let out one horse laugh, yih'see."*

Hot Sun (hot sun) *Noun* – **1.** heat which emanates from the sky, causing dryness, skin irritation, allergic reactions, etc. **2.** concentrated heat from the sun. **3.** bright/hot day. **4.** the bathwater of construction workers. **Eg.** *"It's ah good ting I went school fa accountin' cuz I nah inta goin' out in dah hot sun 'bout poundin' nails."*

Hummuck (huh-muk) *Noun* – **1.** a hammock. **2.** a hanging bed or couch made of canvas, netted cord, or the like, with cords attached to supports at each end. **3.** the best thing to have on the beach hanging between two Willow trees. **Eg.** *"Look, get yoh backside outta my hummuck so I kin lay down n' get some ress."*

Hurtfullest (hert-fuhl-iss) *Adjective* – **1.** the most painful. **2.** full of pain, anguish,; frustration, grief or annoyance. **3.** heartwrenching, disgusting. **Eg.** *"I dunno why Arlette always gah mess wit people man but dah hurtfullest part is dat she already gah one."*

Hh

-idge (idjh) *Suffix/Slang* – **1.** an extension or suffix, which can be added to most words for emphasis. **2.** a creative way of making new words. The suffix 'idge' can be added to many words in very creative ways to develop original slang. For example:

Work-idge:	one's job or workplace or work in general.
Stink-idge:	a really foul odor or an ugly object
Mar-idge:	an extension of the name Mario
Car-idge:	one's automobile
Sleep-idge:	having to sleep, or needing to sleep.
Drunk-idge:	hung over; drunk
Pipe-idge:	a PVC pipe
Rump-idge:	one's buttocks
Funk-idge:	the scent which eminates from one's shoe

...or any such combination of words and phrases using the suffix '–idge'. **Eg.** *"Yeow!! Wah kine ah stink-idge Leroy goin' on wid up in dah bahtchroom man?"*

In Joinin' (in joy-nin) *Adverb* – **1.** cursive handwriting. **2.** to write in flowing strokes with the letters joined together. **3.** a cursive letter or character. **Eg.** *"In penmanship class Miss Joy say I gah good script but I needa practice my in joinin'."*

Ii

In-manly (in-man-leh) *Adjective* – **1.** ill-mannered. **2.** impolite; discourteous; rude. **3.** lacking or indicating a lack of good manners. **Eg.** *"Try so don't bring Kenrick no way wit us. He be goin' on too in-manly, man."*

Iron Shore (eye-urn showre) *Noun* – **1.** the common name for *microkarst*, the eroded, ancient reef structure that forms the shoreline in many areas of the Cayman Islands. **2.** a variety of formations with a common, blackened, jagged appearance. **3.** a shoreline which is comprised primarily of large, spikey, dark rocks made of weathered *dolomite*. **Eg.** *"Goin' fishnin' out on dah iron shore is ah real Cayman tradition."*

Ironwood (eye-yun wood) *Noun* – **1.** (*Chionanthus Caymansis*); a large hardwood tree endemic to the Cayman Islands. **2.** a hard, heavy, strong, and termite-resistant tree. **3.** a tree which was used in old people times to create foundation posts for houses and fence posts for yards and grasspieces. **Eg.** *"Daddy, you tink if dey mek ah boat outta Ironwood it would be bullet proof?"*

It's (ih'tz) *Contraction* – **1.** contraction of *there is*. **2.** it is. **3.** there's. **Eg.** *"You cyah hear when I say it's no more corn meal leff ah wah?"*

Ivan (eye-vun) *Noun* – **1.** Hurricane Ivan. **2.** a category four hurricane which devastated the Cayman Islands for 36 hours in September 2004. **3.** the Great Hurricane of 2004. **4.** one of the worst hurricanes to ever hit the Cayman Islands. **Eg.** *"Since Ivan, all now I nah get my house back t'gedda yet."*

Ivanized (eye-vun-eye-z'd) *Adverb* – **1.** permanently affected or afflicted in some way as a result of Hurricane Ivan. **2.** destroyed by Hurricane Ivan. **3.** flood damaged. **Eg.** *"Even doh gow'ment say 10,000 cars had get Ivanized, it still plenty cars on da road t'day."*

I'yurn (eye-vun-eye-z'd) *Adverb* – **1.** iron. **2.** something hard, strong, rigid, unyielding, or the like. **3.** a really strong metal object. **4.** an instrument used for hot pressing clothes. **Eg.** *"Boy yoh clothes mash up. You nah gah no i'yurn at home ah wah?"* or *"Jed say when he punch Turby in he stomach, it feel like it wah made ouka i'yurn."*

Jew Plum (jew plum) *Noun* – **1.** a type of *'Tahitian apple'* which closely resembles a large guinep, while having a crunchy, tartish meat on the inside. **3.** a favourite Caymanian fruit, whose name is often confused with the 'June Plum'. **Eg.** *"Granfadda, if diss fruit name Jew Plum dah mean I gah be ah Jew ta eat it?"*

John-Joe (jon-joh) *Noun* – **1.** common household mould. **2.** a fungus that produces a superficial growth on various kinds of damp or decaying organic matter. **3.** the green stuff on stale bread and meat. **Eg.** *"Boy, you cyah see dah bread full ah John Joe ah wah? Doon' eat dat."*

Johnny Cake (jaw-neh kaykh) *Noun* – **1.** a large pancake-like bun, similar to a *Fritter*, made from baking soda, butter, salt, flour, etc. and baked in a frying pan. **2.** a frying-pan-sized fritter, which features a heavy crust on the outside, while being soft on the inside. A Johnny Cake is thick and chewy, and allows for 5-6 servings when cut into equal portions. **Eg.** *"Mama, you kin mek meh ah Johnny Cake wit Swanky fa lunch please?"*

Jose's (hoo-sayz) *Noun* – **1.** *Jose's Escape*: a prominent Texaco service station. **2.** a popular gas station located on the corner of Crewe Road and Halfway Pond. **3.** one of the first full-service gas stations in the Cayman Islands. **Eg.** *"I betcha anyting I kin walk from Windsor Park ta Jose's in 20 minutes."*

Juck (juk) *Verb* – **1.** to jerk. **2.** to grab and pull with excessive force. **3.** to draw or haul toward oneself or itself, in a particular direction, or into a particular position. **4.** tug. **Eg.** *"Dah time I went Furdy's widdout acksin' my mama, she jess come juck me out n' errybody wah laffin' at me."*

Juggy (juh-geh) *Noun* – **1.** the largest piece in a sack of playing marbles. **2.** the big marble. **3.** the best marble to use for clearing the ring. **4.** the most vulnerable marble when being called on by an opponent. **Eg.** *"If you see da size ah my juggy yih nah gah waugh play marbles wit me again."*

Jump-Up Church (juhm'p upp chirtch) *Noun* – **1.** any high-spirited church which involves dancing choirs, tambourines, a live-band and/or an interactive audience. **2.** a lively church. **3.** a non-traditional church. **Eg.** *"One time when Joyce-Ann had acks me ta go church, I went wid 'er but I diddn' know it wah gah be ah jump-up church, so I nehva went back."*

June Plum (joon plum) *Noun* – **1.** a type of *'Tahitian Apple'*, closely related to the *'Hog Plum'*, *'Jew Plum'* or *'Golden Apple'* which comes from an equatorial or tropical tree. **2.** a small green fruit which may be eaten raw, although the flesh is crunchy and a little sour. **3.** a favourite Caymanian fruit whose spikey seed can be replanted easily to bear more trees. **Eg.** *"I rememba when dey had ah nice June Plum tree on Goring Avenue b'fore dey bill dah parkin' lot fa Royal Bank."*

Just Minute (juss mih-nitt) *Adverb* – **1.** almost to the minute. **2.** anytime within the last five minutes. **3.** just now. **Eg.** *"How ya mean you bin waitin' long fa me? I just minute came chrew da door n' you wuz'n yah."*

Juug (juug) *Verb* – **1.** to prick. **2.** to puncture with a needle, thorn, or the like. **3.** to jab the body with a pointed object. *Noun* – **4.** a sharp pain caused by or as if by being pricked. **Eg.** *"If you juug me again wit dah pencil I gah tell Teacha McField."*

Keel Out (keele owt) *Verb* – **1.** to stretch out and relax due to fatigue. **2.** laying in a peculiar position. **Eg.** *"My cat always be keel out on da settee in da sittin' room."*

Ketch (ketch) *Verb* – **1.** to catch. **2.** to seize or capture, esp. after pursuit. **3.** to lay hold on. **4.** to check or restrain suddenly. **5.** to attend. **6.** to contract an illness. **Eg.** *"If ya doon' get outta dah rain yih gah ketch ringworm."*

Ketchin' (keh-chin) *Noun* – **1.** a popular game for children whereby two teams draw straws (by counting feet) to decide who will become (A:) the chasers, and who will become (B:) the chasees. The B team is based in a central location (its 'home') with members spread across a large field, while members of the A team roam around hoping to tag a member of the B team before they can make it home. The A team has the power to 'freeze' a member of the B team by touch (tagging). B team members can free their frozen teammates by touching them, which allows them to re-enter the game. If the A team manages to 'freeze' (tag) all members of the B team, the game is over. **Eg.** *"Erry Mondeh mornin' b'fore school, we juss hadda get ah game ah ketchin' ta start da day off."*

Ketchin' News (ketch-in nuze) *Verb* – **1.** getting up to speed on current events through gossip or spying. **2.** sharing the secrets of unsuspecting people. **3.** listening to bad things about good people. **Eg.** *"If ya see Pat n' Alice sittin' down close t'gedda, all dey doin' is ketchin' news."*

Kick Up (kik-up) *Verb* – **1.** to beat up. **2.** to strike violently or forcefully and repeatedly. **3.** to cause painful injury. **4.** to throw a tantrum. **Eg.** *"If you had walk home wit Julio yestaday he wouldn'a get kick up by dem lil' cruffs."*

Kill Out (kihl outt) *Verb* – **1.** to reduce to utter ruin or nonexistence; destroy utterly. **2.** to make extinct. **3.** to annul; make void. **4.** to encroach on the lives of others without regard. **Eg.** *"Fredrick, now you know it nah necessary ta kill out errybody wit yoh stink cologne juss cuz you goin' out wit Petrina t'night."*

Kimmin' (kih-min) *Noun* – From Cayman Brac; **1.** 'Cayman'. **2.** the way *Brackers* pronounce the word *Cayman*. **Eg.** *"I hate when anybody acks me if people from Kimmin' Braick eat soldier crabs fa breakfast."*

Kin (kin) *Auxilliary Verb* – **1.** can. **2.** able to. **3.** having the ability, power, or skill to. **4.** to have the means, qualifications or possibility. **Eg.** *"If he kin do it, I kin do it."*

Kinense Milk (kin-ents milk) *Noun* – **1.** condensed milk. **2.** whole milk reduced by process of evaporation to a thick consistency, with sugar added. **3.** a very thick milk which requires several parts water prior to use. **Eg.** *"Tonight, I gah bayde, comb my hair, and make me ah nice kinense milk sangwich b'fore I go ta bed."*

Kink Neck (keenk nek) *Noun* – **1.** acute soreness in the neck, resulting from a bad sleeping position. **2.** a cramp in the neck. **3.** the result of sleeping on too many pillows or laying in an awkward position for a long time. **Eg.** *"I hadda go check one Kyraprackta dis mornin' cuz I had one bad ole' kink neck lass night n' I couldn' get no sleep."*

Kirk Plaza (kurk plah-zah) *Noun* – **1.** the largest supermarket in central George Town during the 1970s, 80s and 90s. **2.** a large, open parking lot which was formerly used as the hub for many taxis and tour buses when the original supermarket was demolished. **3.** the best place to catch a bus to East End or West Bay in 1990. **Eg.** *"When I used ta liwe Prospect I hadda ketch da 5:15 bus by Kirk Plaza ta get home 5:30."*

Kissin' Up (kih-sin uhpp) *Noun* – **1.** kissing and carressing; necking. **2.** making out. **3.** a popular activity in the early stages of a serious relationship. **Eg.** *"Man, dah time when Miss Julie Ann had find Lesa n' Brenton up in dah Grade 5 closet kissin' up, she turn red like ah lopsta."*

Kk

Kiss Up (kih'ce uhpp) *Verb* – **1.** to brown nose. **2.** to curry favor or behave obsequiously. **3.** to seek favors from a person. **4.** to follow behind someone who has something of value. **5.** to pretend to be interested in one's company. **Eg.** *"I doon' like da way Charlotte had kiss up ta Mista Wight juss so she could get ah bigga cubicle."*

Kite (kyte) *Noun* – **1.** a traditional Caymanian kite, made of brown paper, dried coconut sticks and twine. **2.** a light frame covered with some thin material, to be flown in the wind at the end of a long string. **Eg.** *"Erry summa all ya could see wah dem pretty kite runnin' chrew Mr. Tommy grasspiece."*

Knee Cup (nee kup) *Noun* – **1.** the knee cap. **2.** the flexible part of the leg between the *femur* and the *shin*. **3.** the knee bone. (also called: **Knee Pan**) **Eg.** *"Dah time when Chunky knee cup had come outta place, I nearly faint 'way when I see it"* or; *"Sweety, if any man put he hand on you, juss close yoh eyes and kick im right in he knee pan."*

Knife & Fork (nyfe 'n fawrk) *Noun* – **1.** the name of a road in West Bay, approx. several hundred feet past the West Bay Fire Station. **2.** the former name of the road which is currently called 'Earnest Jackson Drive'. **Eg.** *"I dunno who liwe dong in Knife n' Fork, but if dey house ketch fiyah, dey nah ga hawe worry 'bout fiyah truck getting' deh late."*

Knock Knee (nok nee) *Noun* – **1.** *Genu Valgum:* a condition where the knees angle in and touch one another when the legs are straightened. **2.** an inward curvature of the legs, causing the knees to rub together when walking. **3.** the opposite of bow legs. **Eg.** *"Boy, if you had see Poosey runnin' down Sports Complex wit her knock knee, you woulda had ah good laugh."*

Knotty Head (naw-deh hed) *Noun* – **1.** having a head full of tangled hair. **2.** rugged locks of hair. **3.** an idiot. **Eg.** *"Look ah dah ol' knotty head ting ah Carwell 'eh? I tell im muss mix da cement n' he gone look 'bout paintin'."*

Kunk Out (kunk owt) *Verb* – **1.** to stop working. **2.** to fall into a deep sleep. **3.** to lose consciousness. **4.** to stop operating/functioning. **Eg.** *"Frideh when my car had kunk out on Queen's Highway, I hadda walk 5 miles ta get gas."*

Lady Hair (lay-deh hare) *Noun* – **1.** *Malpigihia cubensis*; a local fern featuring fine hairs that react to human skin like fiberglass. **2.** an innocuous-looking plant which offers a surprise to unwary hikers as the undersides of the leaves have stinging irritating hairs. **3.** a plant which causes misery for anyone who comes in contact with it. **Eg.** *"Mista Burns-eh say he hadda chop out all da lady hair bush in he grasspiece so he grandchildren could play in it."*

Lass (lahce) *Adjective* – **1.** last. **2.** occurring or coming after all others, as in time, order, or place. **3.** being the only one remaining. **4.** the end or conclusion. **Eg.** *"If it's da lass ting I do, I gah clean out dah garage dis weekend."*

Lass Lick (lahce lik) *Noun* – **1.** a popular children's game, where the object is to become the last one to tag the other. **2.** a common cause for children to be beaten with a tamarind switch because they won't get in the car to leave a friend's house. **Eg.** *"Lass week, me n' Turney wah playin' lass lick so much dat I could barely walk the next day."*

Las Tortugas (lahce tawr-too-gus) *Noun* – **1.** the first name given to the Cayman Islands by the famous explorer Christopher Columbus, due to the turtle population on the beach when he arrived. **2.** a word which simply means "the turtles". **Eg.** *"I nehwa even rememba we wah name Las Tortugas until dey had dah Quincentennial ting up by Lion's Centre."*

Late (layte) *Adjective* – **1.** slow to understand. **2.** behind in time. **3.** delayed in reaction. **Eg.** *"Mama, you so late. You didd'n know Mike Tyson had bite piece ah Holyfield ear off?"*

Lazyritis (lay-zeh-rye-dis) *Noun* – **1.** a stroke of sleepiness or fatigue, usually after a large heavy meal. *Verb* – **1.** an uncontrollable need to sleep after eating. *Adverb* – **1.** compelled to sleep. **2.** a zombie-like state due to overeating. **Eg.** *"Anytime lazyritis start sett'n in, ya gah eyeda tek ah nap or go bade quick time ta get rid ah it"*

Lead Bonkey (led boung-keh) *Noun* – **1.** an extremely lazy person. **2.** one who is unable to move due to laziness. **3.** overcome by laziness or fatigue. **Eg.** *"One time when I wah wukkin' dong in Dog City, Shaundell had call me lead bonkey cuz I didd'n waugh do no work."*

Leady (lay-deh) *Noun* – **1.** a playing marble made of metal. **2.** the metal bearing in an empty can of spray paint, which can be cleaned and used as a marble. **3.** the best marble to use in most cases. **Eg.** *"If you see da way my leady mash up he taw, you would'n beliewe it."*

Leguene (leh-gih-nee) *Noun* – **1.** the area behind the Truman Bodden Sports Complex. **2.** a neighborhood located behind the University College of the Cayman Islands. **Eg.** *"My daddy had build nuff nuff houses up in Leguene when he had he own construction company."*

Lemme (leh-mih) *Adverb* – **1.** let me. **2.** to allow or permit. **3.** to allow to pass, go or come. **4.** to cause to; make. **5.** to lend. **Eg.** *"Yow brudda man, lemme ah dolla nah?"*

Lick (lih'k) *Verb* – **1.** to succeed in striking. **2.** to deal a blow or stroke to. **3.** to hit. **4.** to come against with an impact or collision, as a flying fragment, falling body, slap from the hand, or the like. **Eg.** *"Moo from me or else I gah lick you in yoh ol' big lip."*

Lick Up (lih'k upp) *Verb* – **1.** to collide. **2.** to strike one another or one against the other with a forceful impact; come into violent contact; crash. **Eg.** *"Carson! Stop playin' wit dah skateboard in dis house or else one ah deez days yih gah lick up in dah wall n' knock ya teet out."*

Light (lyte) *Adverb* – **1.** having little or no common sense. **2.** gullible or unintelligent. **3.** slow to understand. **4.** unable to comprehend the simplest thing. **Eg.** *"You light boy. You tink I would really set yoh head on fiyah?"*

Lil' Caymanian' (lill kay-mahn'yun) *Noun* – **1.** any person who was either born on Little Cayman or who resides there permanently. **2.** any person from the sister island of Little Cayman. **Eg.** *"Ta be honest I nah meet ah Lil' Caymanian in my life."*

Lion Tongue (ly-un tung) *Noun* – **1.** a thick, greenish coloured shrub, covered in light coloured spots and having a leather-like texture. **2.** a thick leaf, which can used in lieu of a belt during discipline. **Eg.** *"If you eva hear bug somebody gettin' beat wit piece ah Lion Tongue, ya know dey buhind muss be red."*

Liss Tongue (liss tung) *Noun* – **1.** a lisp. **2.** a speech defect consisting in pronouncing *s* and *z* like or nearly like the '*th*' sounds of *thin* and *this*, respectively. **3.** to pronounce or speak with a lisp. **Eg.** *"Mummy, Andrew gah liss tongue n' when he talk, spit be flyin' all up in my mout."*

Log Woods (laowg woodz) *Noun* – **1.** a neighborhood in the district of West Bay located between Hell and Watercourse Road. **2.** an area of West Bay which has been known for its abundance of logwood trees. **Eg.** *"I cyah tell da lass time I went dong in Logwoods, but I nah plannin' go deh no time soon nidda."*

Look Yah (luuk yuh) *Interjection* – **1.** look here. **2.** take a look at this. **3.** have a look. **4.** pay special attention. **5.** see here. **Eg.** *"Boy look yah, you cyah hear stop messin' wit my buggin' CD's ah wah?"*

Long Out (lawng owt) *Verb* – **1.** to stretch. **2.** to draw out or extend. **3.** to extend, spread, or place (something) so as to reach from one point to another. **4.** to hold out; reach forth. **Eg.** *"Babies seem ta always long out dey mout before dey start cryin'."*

Long Wit (lawng witt) *Conjunction* – From Old People Times; **1.** a phrase which is used to identify the relationship of two or more persons. **2.** engaged or married to. **3.** going out with. **Eg.** *"Elmie, tell me something. If Arliss supposed ta be long wit Lucian, how come I see 'er wit Cap'n Curly lass week?"*

Lopsta (lawp-stah) *Noun* – **1.** a lobster. **2.** any of various large, edible, marine, usually dull-green, stalk-eyed decapod crustaceans of the family *Homaridae*, esp. of the genus *Homarus*, having large, asymmetrical pincers on the first pair of legs, one used for crushing and the other for cutting and tearing; the shell turns bright red when cooked. **Eg.** *"Me n' my friend always gah go fa lunch at Lopsta Pot at least once ah week."*

Loud Mout (lowd mowt) *Noun* – **1.** having a big mouth. **2.** a large voice. **3.** having the inability to control one's voice. **4.** a voice which is carried a great distance. **5.** a deep voice. **Eg.** *"You ol' loud mout ting! If I had waugh errybody know my business I woulda print it in da newspaper."*

Lowud (laow-udd) *Adverb* – **1.** the leeward. **2.** the lee side; the point or quarter toward which the wind blows. **3.** the side of something that is sheltered from the wind. **Eg.** *"Dey say dat it's best ta hang yah clothes ta da lowud so dey kin ketch breeze but nah enough dat duss kin blow on um."*

Low Walley (low wah-leh) *Noun* – **1.** the area known as Lower Valley. **2.** a sub-district located between Savannah and Bodden Town, which encompasses Savannah Meadows, Beach Bay and Northward. **3. Eg.** *"I used ta go look fa my friend up in Low Walley but it had get too furd so I stop goin'."*

Luv-in' (luv-inn) *Noun* – **1.** affection. **2.** fond attachment, devotion, or love. **3.** a tender feeling toward another. **Eg.** *"Baby, how come you always gah run off on me and I don't get no luv-in' man?"*

Lyrics (lih-rickz) *Noun, Pl.* – **1.** beautiful words. **2.** having a natural ability to improvise verbally as to convince, or pacify. **3.** the ability to speak convincingly. **4.** a sweet mouth. **Eg.** *"Man, by da time I had finish runnin' da lyrics on dah gyal, her head wah spinnin'."*

Mad Up (mah'd upp) *Verb* – **1.** in an overwhelming state of frustration. **2.** disappointed; thwarted. **3.** unhappy; unsatisfied. **Eg.** *"I doon know wah you sittin' down deh all mad up fah cuz you nah goin' movies wit dem pile ah hooligans I see you runnin' rong wit."*

Mahmah (mah-mah) *Noun* – **1.** one's mother. **2.** the mother of one's children. **3.** the female figure in a traditional family consisting of a *husband, wife* and *children*. **4.** a grandmother who is close to her grandchildren. **Eg.** *"Mahmah Linette, kin me n' Howard go play kite in Misteh Seppy grasspiece?"*

Maiden Plum (may-din pluhm) *Noun* – **1.** *Comocladia Dentata;* Cayman's equivalent to *Poison Ivy*. **2.** a tall, skinny plant, with grapevine-looking leaves, which bears the ability to infect a person with an uncomfortable rash, boils and sores; usually from a great distance; or through prolonged contact with its leaves or milk. **Eg.** *"Don't you go up in dah maiden plum bush 'bout lookin' mangoes. All you gah do is come back all sore up."*

Manchineel Tree (mahn-chi-neel ch'ree) *Noun* – **1.** (*Hippomane mancinella*) a member of the *Euphorbia* family which includes the ornamental *Poinsettia*. **2.** a dangerous plant, due to its milky sap, which is a strong skin irritant; one should never stand under a manchineel to shelter from rain as the oil contains the irritant. **4.** a tree bearing small, green apple-looking fruits which are poisonous to humans, but eaten by the Cayman Blue Iguana. **Eg.** *"Sonny, I know it rainin' but doon' stand unda da Manchineel tree or else it ga strip ya skin off."*

Mango Bush (maiyng-goh) *Noun* – **1.** a large thick brush; usually in a secluded area, where there is an abundance of Mango trees. **2.** a mango jungle. **3.** the area next to a grass piece, containing many mango trees. **Eg.** *"If ya keep gye'n up 'n dah mango bush, yih gah ketch Maiden Plum."*

Man Licks (mahn-likz) *Noun, Pl.* – **1.** strikes or blows which are delivered by a woman with the force and commitment of a man. **2.** to hit as hard as a man. **3.** hard hitting. **Eg.** *"Wheneva Tara used ta get in fights wit her sista, all yih could hear is one whole pile ah man licks ih'nah."*

Mannish (mah-nish) *Adjective* – **1.** being typical or suggestive of a man rather than a woman. **2.** resembling a man, as in size or manner. **Eg.** *"People say Claudette look kinda mannish but I tink she still gah some 'girly-girly' ways."*

Manowar (mahn-a-wawr) *Noun* – **1.** a large bird which spends most of its time soaring above large bodies of water, in search of fish and other game. The body is mostly black, with a long beak, strong, stiff wings and a forked tail. **2.** the large black birds often seen circling over the beachside fish market near North Church Street. **Eg.** *"Wheneva ya go out fishin' in a boat, it good ta look up cuz if yih see manowars circlin' dah mean fish close ta da surface."*

Man Shoes (mahn shooze) *Noun* – **1.** a young boy's interpretation of very elegant dress shoes which resemble those that a man would wear to work or church. **2.** hard shoes. **3.** a boy's dress shoes. **Eg.** *"Lass week Satday, Mama mek me an Kirwin put on uwah man shoes so we cun go walkin' out in tong."*

Marina (mah-ree-nah) *Noun* – **1.** a man's white, sleeveless undershirt. **2.** a tight-fitting tank top. **3.** a close-fitting, low-cut top having shoulder straps and often made of lightweight, knitted fabric. **Eg.** *"If ya go outside een ah marina, dem miskittas gah have ya all bite up in no time."*

Marl Road (mah'rl rode) *Noun* – **1.** the word on the street. **2.** hearsay. **3.** what people are saying. **4.** the latest news or gossip. **5.** a road made of marl. **Eg.** *"I just goin' by marl road still. People say Shekira used ta check Rodney, but she get ketch kissin' Larden ova by Marcella house. Wahhename nearly kick Larden ta pieces n' he run home ta he mama."*

May Cow (mey kow) *Noun* – **1.** a folklore created by early farmers on the island of Cayman Brac to keep children away from the mango trees. **2.** a ghost story similar to the *Rolling Calf*, and derived from lower Caribbean bedtime stories. **3.** an old wives fable featuring a mythical cow-like creature with fiery red eyes, stripes on its body, and a large chain around its neck. **4.** a ghost story created to scare children to sleep. **5.** a form of 'duppy' (spirit), which is also referred to as *Willgo, Old Willie Go, Rolling Calf* and *Roaring Calf*. **Eg.** *"Loyce Ann say when she wah small, if you had tell her May Cow wah comin', she wah in dah bed n' out like ah light before you could cunk ta tree."*

Meat Kind (meet kine) *Noun* – **1.** any type of meat that is the focal point of a traditional Caymanian meal. **2.** roast beef, Cayman-Style Beef, curry chicken, pork, spare ribs, etc. **3.** an order of cooked meat that is accompanied by several sides, including rice, cole slaw, and potatoes. **Eg.** *"You nah gah have no meat kind wit yoh dinna, Mr. Frank?"*

Meckin' Down (mehk-in dawng) *Verb* – **1.** approaching. **2.** of the relative near future. **3.** the event of one object coming closer to another. **4.** the temporal property of becoming nearer in time. **5.** the act of drawing spatially closer to something. **Eg.** *"Boy, try so hurry n' nail up dah plywood on dem windows. You cyah see bad wedda meckin' down now ah wah?"*

Michette (mih-shet, mah-chet or mah-sheet) *Noun* – **1.** a common household machete. **2.** a large heavy knife used esp. in Caribbean countries in cutting sugar cane and clearing underbrush and as a weapon. **3.** the weapon of choice for most fights during the 1990s. **Eg.** *"One time Carlos had tell me 'bout how he wah diggin' ah hole wit he michette ta plant yams n' he slice he foot open on da blade."*

M'lowe (mih'luwe) *Noun* – From West Bay; **1.** my love. **2.** my sweetheart. **3.** my friend. **Eg.** *"M'lowe, you cyah get me some wadda t'drink ah wah?"*

Mindin' Baby (myne-in bay-beh) *Verb* – **1.** attending to a young baby. **2.** taking care of one's child. **3.** watching over a crib or bed while a baby sleeps. **4.** staying home to take care of one's child. **Eg.** *"Wah in dah world you know about mindin' baby?"*

Mines (mynez) *Pronoun, Pl.* – **1.** belonging to oneself. **2.** the nominative singular pronoun used by a speaker in referring to himself or herself. **Eg.** *"I kinda like da way yoh dog look, but mines look betta, still."*

Miskittas (miss-kid-uz) *Noun, Pl.* – **1.** mosquitos. **2.** any of numerous dipterous insects of the family *Culicidae*, the females of which suck the blood of animals and humans, some species transmitting certain diseases, as *malaria* and *yellow fever*. **Eg.** *"I ready fah dem miskittas t'night. I gah my smoke pan, my miskitta stick, my fly swat, fly paper, n' da 'fogga commin' chrew 'rong 'bout sebb'm-a-clock."*

Miss Ma'am (mih'ss ma'ahm) *Noun* – **1.** a young lady who may have the tendency of behaving like an older woman. **2.** a very mature female child. **Eg.** *"Yeh, miss ma'am. Ya tink cuz ya gettin' ready fah college now ya kin run 'bug all time ah night wit God knows who, doin' who knows what?"*

Mista Man (mihs-tah mahn) *Noun* – **1.** a young boy or teenager who has the tendency to behave as if he were an adult. **2.** a boy who does not know his place. **3.** a phrase used to identify a young boy who is in trouble. **Eg.** *"Yeah Mista Man. So you feel you ah big shot now cuz you win all kinda track n' feel trophies lass munt? Well, I gah show you who still boss; ya grounded till dah end ah da munt!"*

Misteh (miss-teh) *Noun* – From Old People Times; **1.** mister. **2.** a conventional title of respect for a man, prefixed to the name and to certain official designations. **Eg.** *"Misteh Frank always seem ta stop 'bout diss muchness from da garage wall. Ah know he brave."*

Miya Zwell (my-ah-z'well) *Adverb* – **1.** a consolidation of the phrase "may as well". **2.** to disregard conventional methods. **3.** to go ahead; regardless of the outcome. **Eg.** *"I know it gah be hard, but we miya zwell break up now, cuz we nah gettin' along, n' I doo' waugh nuttin' more ta do wit you."*

MLA (em elle aye) *Noun* – **1.** an elected Member of the Legislative Assembly. **2.** one of over a dozen elected members of the Assembly which represents the Islands' six voting districts. **3.** a Cayman politician. **Eg.** *"Kurwell say anytime anybody be messin' wit he cows, he jess go check ah MLA n' dey try dey bess ta sort it out fah im."*

Mm

Mout (mowt) *Noun* – **1.** one's mouth. **2.** the opening through which an animal or human takes in food. **3.** the oral cavity considered as the source of vocul utterance. **4.** the area of the human body which includes the lips, jaw, tongue, and teeth. **Eg.** *"Hush ya mout! You cyah hear wah I say ah wah?"*

Muchness (mutch-niss) *Adverb* – **1.** a measure of distance between two objects or places. **2.** quantity, or degree. **3.** an approximate measurement. **3.** just about. **4.** relative closeness. **Eg.** *"Wah Jermaine kickin' up all kine ah fuss fah? All I tek is 'bout diss muchness ah he lemonade."*

Muhbee (muh-bee) *Helping Verb* – From East End; **1.** must be. **2.** obliged or bound by an imperative requirement. **3.** compelled to either fulfill some need or to achieve an aim. **Eg.** *"Boy, you muhbee stchupid if you tink I gah lend ya my new fishin' line ta go out on dah iron shore."*

Mummah (muh-maah) *Noun* – **1.** one's mother. **2.** a grandmother. **3.** an older mother. **4.** a grandmother who is close to her grandchildren. **Eg.** *"Juss acks yah mummah n' she kin tell ya how we used ta play when we wah small."*

Mussle Up (muss-el up) *Adverb* – **1.** very muscular. **2.** of or pertaining to muscle or the muscles. **3.** having very well-developed muscles; brawny. **4.** resembling a bodybuilder. **Eg.** *"Man, you shoulda see how Lennox wah all mussle up dah time when he wah trainin' fah dah bodybuildin' championships."*

My Lil' Friend (mye lil fren) *Pronoun* – **1.** a woman's close male friend. **2.** a woman's pet name for a young man who is too young to start a relationship with, but still a close friend. **3.** a male security guard or store clerk who has a close personal relationship with a woman. **Eg.** *"Try so leave my lil' friend alone nah? He nah no hurt ta nobody."*

My Sweetums (mye swee-dum'z) *Pronoun* – **1.** a nickname for a young baby. **2.** an expression of passion or excitement for something cute; as in a young baby. **Eg.** *"Look ah my sweetums eh? I lowe he lil' pretty eyes."*

Mm

Naah (na'ah) *Adverb* – **1.** no. **2.** a negative used to express dissent, denial, or refusal, as in response to a question or request. **3.** an utterance of the word "no". **4.** to reject, refuse approval, or express disapproval of. **Eg.** *"Wah? Naah. I know it could'n ah go like daht or else I would'n be yah right now."*

Nable (nay-bull) *Noun* – **1.** one's navel; belly button. **2.** the central point or middle of any thing or place. **3.** the mark on the surface of the abdomen of mammals where the umbilical cord was attached during gestation. **Eg.** *"Aye, you doon' see yoh nable showin' ah wah? Try so go put on ah longa blouse."*

Nah (n'uh) *Adverb* – **1.** not. **2.** a word used to express negation, denial, refusal, or prohibition. **3.** in no way; to no degree. **4.** absolutely not. **Eg.** *"I guess I gah have ta try harda from now on or else I nah gah get da raise I need ta pay my mortgage."*

Nai'ema (nye-eh-muh) *Adverb* – **1.** won't even. **2.** will not. **3.** more than likely will not. **Eg.** *"If ah nudda hurricane strike Cayman, we nai'ema gah hawe worry bug nuttin' cuz we already know how deal wid it now."*

Needlecase (nee-dul kayce) *Noun* – **1.** the *Dragonfly*. **2.** any of numerous stout-bodied, nonstinging insects of the order *Odonata* (suborder *Anisoptera*), the species of which prey on mosquitoes and other insects and are distinguished from the damselflies by having the wings outstretched rather than folded when at rest. **Eg.** *"Gee! I know da way ya see ah whole pile ah needlecase."*

Nn

Neese Berry (neeze beh-reh) *Noun* – **1.** the *Naseberry*. **2.** the fruit of the sapodilla, *Manilkara zapota*. **3.** the *sapodilla* tree. **4.** an evergreen tree of the Caribbean and Central America, having latex that yields chicle and edible fruit with sweet yellow-brown flesh. **Eg.** *"Aye, come so pick meh one neese berry nah? Ma back hurtin' from playin' football."*

Nehwah (neh-wah) *Adverb* – **1.** never. **2.** not ever; at no time. **3.** not at all; absolutely not. **4.** to no extent or degree. **Eg.** *"Daddy! You rememba da lass time you say you wah gah cyar me fishnin' n' you nehwah did it? We kin go diss Easta instead?"*

Nehwah Happin' (neh-wah hap-in) *Adjective* – **1.** no way. **2.** not now, not ever. **3.** forget it. **Eg.** *"Uh-ugh! Nehwah happin'! You tink you kin jess come in my room n' run my a/c n' I wuzz'n gah say nuttin? You muss be mad."*

Nevyew (neh'v-yoo) *Noun* – **1.** one's nephew. **2.** the son of one's sister or brother. **3.** a son of one's spouse's brother or sister. **4.** a special child. **Eg.** *"I like ta watch my lil' nevyew (nephew) sleepin' yih'see?"*

New Brand (nyoo bran) *Adjective* – **1.** 'brand new'. **2.** entirely new. **3.** completely new. **4.** a recent purchase which is in immaculate condition. **Eg.** *"Erry time dey have ah reggae concert, Kursley always gah buy ah new brand pair ah shoes ta go out wit yih'nah?"*

Newlands (nyoo-lundz) *Noun* – **1.** a sub-district of Savannah. **2.** the housing community which surrounds the International College of the Cayman Islands, and the Rackley Canal. **3.** a quiet and peaceful place to live. **Eg.** *"If you cun hitch all a way Prospect, you cun hitchin' lil furda an reach Newlands, still"* or; *"I hear dem people from Newlands lowe country music and raise cows fa fun."*

Nickas (nih-kuhz) *Noun, Pl.* – **1.** a group of small, dark gray seeds, mostly flat or odd-shaped; which become hot when rubbed against a hard surface, such as concrete. **2.** hot seeds, which young boys use to burn eachother as a practical joke. **3.** a group of gray seeds from the *Cock Spur* plant, which tend to grow in the wild thickets throughout the Islands. **Eg.** *"Miss Junilee say she gah fix Lil' Frankie fah puttin' dem nickas down in da back ah her pants suit."*

Nidda (nih-duh) *Conjunction* – **1.** neither; not either, as of persons or things specified. **2.** not one or the other. **3.** not one person or the other; not one thing or the other. **Eg.** *"Bobo tell me something? You nah gah nidda season salt we kin use ta mek 'sauce' fah deez green maiyngah's?"*

Nize (nyze) *Noun* – **1.** sound, esp. of a loud, harsh, or confused kind. **2.** a disturbance, especially a random and persistent disturbance, that obscures or reduces the clarity of a signal. **Eg.** *"Aye man! Stop mekkin' nize wit dah car fa I tell yoh daddy."*

Noblin (naw'b-lin) *Noun* – **1.** having a large nob (a bulbous protrusion) on the back of one's head. **2.** a round head. **3.** a big head. **Eg.** *"Gee, look ah dah piece ah noblin you gah deh man? I know you mussa gah nuff brains, still."*

No-Nuttin' (noh nutt'n) *Adverb* – **1.** an insignificant person or thing. **2.** a nobody. **3.** unimportant, trifling, or petty. **4.** too small to be important. **5.** of no consequence, influence, or distinction. **Eg.** *"You expeck ta put one ol' no-nuttin against Manchesta n' wonda how come dey lose? You bin smokin' breadfruit leaf ah wah?"*

Norrud (naw-rud) *Noun* – **1.** to the north. **2.** a cardinal point of the compass, lying in the plane of the meridian and to the left of a person facing the rising sun. **3.** in, toward, or facing, the north. **Eg.** *"Bobo, look yah, I bin ah Sea Captain now fah twenny fiwe years, so if I say pint da boat ta da norrud, dah mean we goin' Miami. Undastand?"*

Nor'Side (nawr'syde) *Noun* – **1.** the district of North Side. **2.** one of Grand Cayman's 5 districts. **3.** the area consisting of Frank Sound, a part of Old Man Bay, the Hutland, Rum Point, Cayman Kai, and Kaibo. **Eg.** *"If yah waugh talk 'bout ah good place ta relax jess go Nor'side an chill out on da beach."*

Nor'westa (nawr-wess-tah) *Noun* – **1.** a wind or gale from the northwest. **2.** a storm or gale blowing from the northwest. **3.** a really windy storm which brings rain and high tides to shore. **Eg.** *"Anytime ya see nor'westa comin' ya bedda board up ya windows or else ya roof might blow off."*

Nn

No Teet (noh-teet) *Noun* – **1.** having little or no teeth **2.** a person with very few teeth. **3.** toothless. **Eg.** *"Mista Fred is da ownliss man wit one ol' no teet dog det bark wid ah lisp."*

No Way (noh whey) *Adverb* – **1.** nowhere. **2.** in or at no place; not anywhere. **3.** being or leading nowhere; pointless; futile. **4.** not the best way. **Eg.** *"I waugh go happy hour Frideh cuz I nah bin no way in monts."*

Nuff (nuh'f) *Adjective* – **1.** enough. **2.** adequate for the want or need; sufficient for the purpose or to satisfy desire. *Adverb* – **3.** an adequate quantity or number; sufficiency. **4.** fully or quite. **Eg.** *"Wahght! You gah nuff mangoes, doh. Set me up wit one ah dem nah?"*

Numbers (num-buz) *Noun* – **1.** an underground lottery, which involves several members placing bets prior to a raffle, of which one (or sometimes more than one) winner is selected. **2.** illegal gambling. **Eg.** *"Aye, you nah hear which numba play dis week ah wah? I waugh see who win da $5,000.00."*

Numb Fish (numm fish) *Noun* – **1.** a small, shell-covered fish, bearing a thick, scaley hide, covered in bumps for protection and spikes for stinging predators and prey. **2.** a really ugly fish, which burrows itself in the sand to ambush its prey and hide from predators. **3.** one of the many legends that most people in Cayman have never seen. **Eg.** *"Sweetie, watch out way you walkin' in da sea, y'hear? Somebody tell me Freddy get sting by Numbfish cupple ah weeks ago, rite in diss spot."*

Nuttin' (nuh-t'n) *Noun* – **1.** nothing. **2.** no thing; not anything. **3.** no part, share or trace. **4.** something that is non existent. **Eg.** *"Man, if you nah doin' nuttin' t'night, try so less go by Buttonwood n' shoot some pool nah?"*

Nuune (noon) *Noun* – (primarily of East End and Bodden Town) **1.** none. **2.** no one; not one. **3.** not any, as of something indicated. **4.** not at all or in no way. **Eg.** *"Doon' acks me fah money agin cuz I nah gah nuune ta gi you."*

Nn

Old Cayman House (oal kay-mahn how'ce) *Noun* – **1.** a traditional house built in the old style, and made of wattle and daub or wood and having a zink roof. **2.** the type of home one's grandparents might currently live in. **Eg.** *"Ta get ta Miss LuLu house, jess go dong by Uncle Kirwin guinep tree, turn leff, den go down chrew Misteh Larden grass piece, and den yih gah come up ta one pink n' white old Cayman house on piece ah iron shore... dass Miss LuLu house."*

One English Man (wun eeng-lish mahn) *Noun* – **1.** any person whose origins lie in the United Kingdom, whether it be from the Island of England, Scotland or Ireland. **2.** a Brit. **3.** any man with an English accent. **Eg.** *"Man, I hear one English man had get ketch committin' fraud on dah Eurobank case."*

One Lil' Man (wun lill mahn) *Noun* – **1.** a really short fellow who shows up at one's home or place of business unannounced, while one is absent. **2.** a really short guy. **3.** an individual who can only be identified by his height and body type. **4.** a man who cannot be fully identified by the message taker, because no name or other form of identification was given at the time of the visit. **Eg.** *"Joy, one lil' man juss came see you but I diddn' know way u wuz."* or; *"I know Hurley had tell you det Radley get mash up in ah car accident cuz he wah drunk but it nehwa happen like dat. Dey say one lil' man wah drivin' ah dump truck n' run off da road cuz he wah gazin' at some ol' big bunkey gyal."*

One Piece (wun peece) *Prefix* – **1.** a nonspecific reference to objects, events or activities. **2.** a lot of one thing. **Eg.** *"I see dah time when Lillian had fall offa her brudda bicycle, she start one piece ah hollarin' n' errybody juss come runnin' like somebody wah dead."*

Oo

One Tourist Man (wun tore-iss mahn) *Noun* – **1.** a male tourist. **2.** any male person who is new to the Islands and knows very little about its culture. **3.** a man who has the tendency of showing up in a restaurant dressed in swim trunks and no shirt. **Eg.** *"One time I see one tourist man come up in Corna acksin' fa directions ta Westin, n' da cashier tell im West End is in Cayman Brac."*

One Tourist Woman (wun tore-iss wuh'mun) *Noun* – **1.** a female tourist. **2.** any female person who is new to the Islands and knows very little about its culture. **3.** a woman who has the tendency of showing up in front of one's home asking for directions while riding on the back of a scooter. **Eg.** *"Man, if you had see dah piece ah bikini one tourist woman had on lass week, yoh eyes woulda fall outta yoh head."*

Ouk (owhk) *Adverb* – **1.** out. **2.** away from, or not in, the normal or usual place, position, state, etc. **3.** not in present possession or use, as on loan. **4.** not in. **Eg.** *"Mummy! Tell Carson ta hurry up n' come ouk ah da bahtchroom or else I gah pee-pee up myself."*

Out House (owt how'ce) *Noun* – **1.** a small tool shed or storage facility to the rear of a dwelling home. **2.** an old Cayman-style bathroom made of wood built over a large pit, which houses one or more crudely made toilet seats. **Eg.** *"I used to hate goin' down by my granny's cuz all she had wah one ol' out house n' I had always get stuck in deh wit no tylet paypah."*

Ouwa (uh-wah) *Pronoun* – **1.** our; a nominative plural of 'I' used to denote oneself and another or others. **2.** a form of the possessive case of *'we'* used as an attributive adjective. **3.** belonging to us. **Eg.** *"It's ah good ting ouwa house nehwa blow down durin' Ivan cuz we wouldn' ah had no way ta stay."*

Ownliss (ooon-liss) *Adverb* – **1.** only. **2.** without others or anything further; alone; solely; exclusively. **3.** no more than; merely; just. **4.** being the single one or the relatively few of the kind. **Eg.** *"Sicily is da ownliss friend I gah det really care 'bout how I doin'."*

Oo

Padnah (pah'd-nuh) *Noun* – **1.** a financial partnership between two or more persons, which involves the pooling together of funds. **2.** one of the best ways to raise a large sum of money for a particular cause. **3.** to contribute money to a shared transaction. **Eg.** *"Man, one time I jine one padnah n' draw out $8,000 one lick yih'nah."*

Padnah Ground (pah'd-nuh graown) *Noun* – From Old People Times; **1.** the property - off of Elgin Avenue - which belonged to the former Racquet Club sports bar. **2.** the area on which the new Government Office is currently located. **Eg.** *"Dem times when we used ta play football up by Agriculture Field, we used ta hawe ta cut chrew by Padnah Ground ta get home b'fore dark."*

Pah (pa'ah) *Noun* – **1.** one's father. **2.** daddy. **3.** a male guardian. **Eg.** *"Sonny, go so call ya pah fah meh nah? I waugh acks im if he kin' gimme ah drop dong da road."*

Palm Dale (pah'm day'le) *Noun* – **1.** a housing community off of Crewe Road near to Tropical Gardens. **3.** a quiet neighborhood near the airport. **Eg.** *"Jeremy say as long as he live he gah represent Palm Dale like it da bible."*

Paper Towellin' (pay-pah tow-ill-inn) *Noun* – **1.** paper towel: a disposable towel made of absorbent paper. **Eg.** *"Archie, come so run by Merren shop 'n get me some Windex n' some paper towellin'."*

Pahpa (pah-puh) *Noun* – **1.** one's grandfather. **2.** an older man who has a tendency to interfere with the raising of his grandchildren. **3.** the father of one's father. **4.** a link to one's family heritage and tradition. **Eg.** *"I rememba when my pahpa had mek me one stool ta sit on wit he bare hands."*

Pahro (pah-row) *Adverb* – **1.** of, like, or suffering from *paranoia*. **3.** very uneasy; untrusting. *Noun* – **4.** a person suffering from *paranoia*. **Eg.** *"Boy you pahro. You cyah hear deh nah no such ting as duppy ah wah?"*

Pain Up (pee'n upp) *Adverb* – **1.** physically painful or sensitive, as a wound, hurt, or diseased part. **2.** sore; tender; infected; wounded. **3.** full of aches and pains. **Eg.** *"I love workin' out in da gym y'see? Aftawords ya be all pain up, but afta ya bade it feel good."*

Painy Belly (pee-neh beh-leh) *Noun* – **1.** pain in the stomach caused by gas or cramps. **2.** an ache in the abdomen. **3.** a reason to complain through whining or moaning. **Eg.** *"Diss mornin' I had one painy belly like ah dunno wah... I taught I wah gah die."*

Patty (pah-deh) *Noun* – **1.** a traditional Cayman-style meat pastry. **2.** any item of food covered with dough, batter, etc., and fried or baked. **Eg.** *"You rememba when we used ta go get ah patty n' ah pepsi from Island Taste when dey wah on da waterfront?"*

Picky Head (pih-keh hed) *Noun* – **1.** the state of one's hair which closely resembles a bush; thick and shaggy. **2.** untidy; unkempt hair. **3.** overgrown and poorly groomed hair. **Eg.** *"Aaaaahhhh!! Look ah yoh ol' picky head dog man? Way you get him from?"*

Pint (pynt) *Verb* – **1.** to point. **2.** to stress a particular topic or part of a story. *Noun* – **3.** a sharp or tapered end. **4.** a mark or dot used in printing or writing for punctuation, especially a period. **5.** a reason. **Eg.** *"Errytime Linford try tell ah story, Gina always gah im ta get ta da pint."*

Pirates Week (py-rutz week) *Noun* – **1.** an annual festival held in recognition of Pirates who first visited the Islands during the 17 and 1800's. **2.** a grand event, comprising of a costumed street parade, a pantomime, a street dance, a fireworks display, and lots of other activities for the whole family; held in November of each year. **Eg.** *"Nex year I gye'n Pirates Week dress like Captain Jack Sparrow."*

Pp

Piss Pot (pih'ce pawt) *Noun* – **1.** a large round pot or bowl, made of porcelain or metal, which is used during urination. **2.** a portable toilet bowl. **3.** an old Cayman toilet. **Eg.** *"Watch ya? Boy if you had turn ova dah piss pot, I woulda mek you wipe up erry lass drop b'fore you go school."*

Plaitin' (plahtt'n) *Verb* – **1.** to braid or plait anything, especially thatch, coconut leaves, or straw. **2.** the act of braiding one's hair or other material. **3.** a favourite pastime for older Caymanian women. **Eg.** *"My Aunt Miriam cun do some plaitin' doh yi'nah."*

Plantain Trash Bed (plah'n-t'n trah'sh bade) *Noun* – **1.** a traditional Caymanian bed (from the late 19th and early 20th century) which bears a mattress made from the leaves of a *Plantain Sucker* tree. **2.** a a very soft mattress made of plantain leaves. **Eg.** *"Granny say deez new beds cyah touch da plantain trash beds she used ta mek back in her good ol' days."*

Playin' Karate (play-yin kah-rah-deh) *Verb* – **1.** pretending to fight with the skills of a true martial artist. **2.** imitating key kung fu movie characters such as Bruce Lee, Jet Li or Jackie Chan. **3.** getting your butt kicked by your next door neighbor. **Eg.** *"Next time me n' you playin' karate I gah fly kick you inside yoh head fa bussin' my lip da lass time."*

Playin' Up (play-yin upp) *Adverb* – **1.** frolicking; having fun; flirting. **2.** messing around. **3.** clowning. **Eg.** *"Aye, get outta my room n' stop playin' up in people bed like it yours!"*

Play Toy (pley toi) *Noun* – **1.** one's toy. **2.** a play thing. **3.** a doll; baseball; CD; videogame; or other object used for the entertainment of oneself. **4.** an object, often a small representation of something familiar as an animal or person for children or others to play with. **Eg.** *"People mussa tink dah car is yoh play toy da way you treat it."*

Plywood Bunkey (plie wud bung-keh) *Noun* – **1.** buttocks which are as flat as a piece of plyboard. **2.** having wide buttocks which appear to be completely flat. **3.** a flat butt. **4.** no bonkey whatsoever. **Eg.** *"I hear Robby checkin' one gyal dat gah ah serious piece ah plywood bonkey boy."*

Poinciana Tree (pun-see-yah-nuh tree) *Noun* – **1.** any of several other tropical trees of the legume family, with showy flowers. **2.** a really huge tree which bears bright red-orange petals several times a year. **3.** a very messy tree to have in one's yard. **Eg.** *"I really like dah pictcha wit dem two Poinciana trees crossin' ova da road in Sawannah while dey bloomin'; dass ah nice one ta put on da wall."*

Pomp (pawmp) *Verb* – **1.** to emit, cause or produce a honk. **2.** to cause an automobile horn to sound. **3.** the blaring sound of the horn from a motor vehicle. **Eg.** *"I really don't care if you go head and pomp yo horn till kingdom come, I nah movin my car till you get yo ol' jalopy out da way."*

Pong (pawng) *Noun* – **1.** a measurement; one pound. **2.** a very foul odor; a stench. *Verb* – **3.** to strike an object by delivering blows to it from overhead; to pound. **Eg.** *"I hear Tee-Cee had get pong up by Chelsea dah time in highschool."*

Poomp (poo'mp) *Noun* – **1.** a 'fart'. **2.** a flatus expelled through the anus. *Verb* – **3.** to break wind. **4.** to relieve flatulence and release a very foul, offensive smelling odor. **5.** to make a funny sound with one's behind. **Eg.** *"One time Fletch had poomp durin' ah all-school meetin' n' dey hadda clear da buildin' like it wah on fiyah."*

Pop Head (pawp hed) *Noun* – **1.** an injury to the top of the head which results in splitting of the skin and bleeding. **2.** an insult. **3.** a very painful head injury. **Eg.** *"I rememba one time when Baby Frank hadda get 17 stitches ta close up he pop head."*

Pop Lip (pawp lipp) *Noun* – **1.** an injury to the mouth which results in a splitting of the skin and bleeding. **2.** the result of being punched hard, in the mouth. **3.** a swollen lip which has been injured in some way. **Eg.** *"Ted had come school one day wid ah pop lip da size ah Cayman Brac Bluff when he Daddy slap im fah lyin'!"*

Poppy Show (paw-peh sho) *Verb* – **1.** to show off. **2.** to purposely attract attention to oneself. **3.** to slave for the impression of others. **4.** to act the fool. **Eg.** *"Jason get ah poppy show dah time 'bout doin stunts on he bicycle 'n bring up inside ah Mista Curly chicken coop. I nearly dead laffin'!"*

Pretty Eye (prih-deh eye) *Adjective* – **1.** having very attractive eyes. **2.** having either hazel, blue, gray or light brown eyes. **3.** eyes which are magnetic and appealing. **Eg.** *"Keisha say if she decide ah go prom diss year, it gah only be wit one pretty eye boy name Harley."*

Prickle Bush (prih-k'l buush) *Noun* – **1.** any area containing dense portions of trees and plants which are at least 60-80% covered in prickles or thorns. **2.** a dried out thicket, filled with thorns or prickles, and having very few leaves or shrubbery. **Eg.** *"Wah you hadda go up in dah prickle bush fah when I tell you not to?"*

Prickly Gut (prihk-leh gut) *Noun* – **1.** the whitish-coloured stomach of a Green Sea Turtle. The prickly gut is removed during butchering and resembles a porcupine, hence the name 'prickly'. **2.** a favourite delicacy among turtle product enthusiasts. **Eg.** *"Wheneva I used ta watch daddy cut out da prickly gut, I used ta feel like I wah goin' chrow up. It juss look nasty, man."*

Proudy (praow-deh) *Adverb* – **1.** drawn to self-actualization. **2.** having, proceeding from, or showing a high opinion of one's own dignity, importance, or superiority. **3.** full of vanity. **4.** stuck up. **5.** snobbish. **Eg.** *"Ol' proudy, always gah be different eh?"*

Puhpah (puh-paah) *Noun* – From West Bay; **1.** one's grandfather. **2.** an older man who constantly interferes with the raising of his grandchildren. **3.** the father of one's father. **Eg.** *"If you doon' get outta my ya'ad rike now, I gah call my puhpah on you."*

Pupaw (puh-pawe) *Noun* – **1.** the *Papaya* fruit. **2.** a large, yellow, melon-like fruit of a tropical shrub or small tree, *Carica papaya*, eaten raw or cooked. **3.** a large oval melon-like tropical fruit with yellowish flesh. **Eg.** *"In some places, dey call it papaya, but Caymanians call it pu-paw. I doon' care wah yah call it cuz I gah eat it same way."*

Pp

Quadrille (kwawh-drih'lle) *Noun* – **1.** a traditional square dance for four couples, consisting of five parts or movements, each complete to itself. **2.** the music for such a dance. **3.** a favourite dance of the fashionable French society in the late 18th century, which debuted in the ballrooms of England in the early 19th century, from where it found its way into various European dependencies, such as the West Indies. **4.** a Cayman tradition which was preserved for many years by Radley Gourzong and the Happy Boys band. **Eg.** *"At Agriculture Fair dis year, da East End Quadrille Troup had errybody all rile up n' dancin' all on top da tables n' ting; boy dah way ya see people hawin' fun."*

Quashy (k'wash-eh) *Noun* – **1.** a really insignificant person. **2.** a worthless individual. **3.** a person of little significance, importance, or one who appears to possess no skills or talents whatsoever. **Eg.** *"Daddy used ta get mad anytime he wah watchin' wresslin' n' dey put ah ol' quashy in ta fight wit da World Champion. He say it wah ah waste ah time juss ta watch it."*

Queen's Highway (k'ween'z hi-waye) *Noun* – **1.** the road linking North Side and East End, which was opened during the Royal Visit of Queen Elizabeth II in February 1983. A plaque commemorating the event was placed at the site. **2.** one of the only places on the island where the speed limit is 50mph. **3.** a long stretch of open road that is attractive to speeders. (many fatal accidents have taken place on Queen's Highway) **Eg.** *"Anytime I hear bug ah accident, da first ting dat come ta my mind is "I betcha it happin' on Queen's Highway."*

Quenk (kweh'nk) *Noun* – **1.** a sound. **2.** the utterance or emission of a squeak or squeaky sound. **3.** any sound which can be heard. **Eg.** *"Alright you children, it bedtime now, so unnna go ta bed n' I doon' waugh hear ah quenk or else I gah bring da belt."*

Que-Que (kyoo-kyoo) *Noun* – **1.** a small quantity (mostly of a drink), such as a shot of liquor. In relation to spirits it tends to refer to a small unmeasured quantity. **2.** one of the three legal sizes for draught beer glasses; it was formerly used for very strong beer but is now rarely seen. **3.** a small hard liquor flask usually kept in the back pocket during times of celebration. **Eg.** *"Erry Christmas, pahpa hadda hawe he que-que in he back pocket so if he friends come ova he would hawe something ta drink."*

Quick Time (kweh-heh) *Adverb* – **1.** quickly. **2.** immediately. **3.** at once. **4.** right away. **5.** on the double. **6.** right now. **7.** with speed; rapidly; very soon. **Eg.** *"Less go drop diss off deez tapes ta Blockbusta quick time while dey still open nah?"*

Quincentennial (kwin-sen-ten-ih-yul) *Noun* – **1.** 2003; the 500th anniversary of the discovery of the Cayman Islands by Christopher Columbus on May 10, 1503. **2.** a very memorable year for the people of the Cayman Islands. **Eg.** *"Quincentennial year was ah really beautiful celebration for Cayman. I think Angela Martins did ah excellent job puttin' erryting tagedda."*

Qweh-heh (kweh-heh) *Adjective* – **1.** nothing at all. **2.** having no knowledge of anything. **3.** lacking proper understanding or knowledge. **4.** completely oblivious. **Eg.** *"Look yah right? Tracey Ann always try ta show me up in uwah staff meetin's but she doon' know qweh-heh 'bug Accountin' n' I almost gah my CPA."*

Qq

Rain Fly (reen flye) *Noun* – **1.** a small brown flying termite commonly seen during or after a long rain. **2.** a harmless moth-like fly. **3.** an annoying but unoffensive insect. **Eg.** *"If ya see ah rain fly pitch on yoh pillow when ya wake up in da mornin', dah usually mean it rain hard da night b'fore."*

Rat Trap (raht traapp) *Noun* – **1.** an old, beat-up, shabby, dilapidated, tetanus infected automobile, which appears to have lived past its time. **2.** a junk-mobile. **3.** a jalopy. **Eg.** *"Cuzzy, if you had see dah rat trap way Binwurd daddy gi him ta drive, you woulda ketch diarrhea in yo pants."*

Rebecca's Cave (rih-beh-kuhz kay'v) *Noun* – **1.** a large cave located in the West End district of Cayman Brac, where a young girl named Rebecca took shelter and died during the 1932 hurricane. **2.** a famous attraction on Cayman Brac. **Eg.** *"Dah time when dem children had skip school n' went beer drinkin' up in Rebecca's Cave, I know dey mussa get ah good beatin' dah day."*

Red Ade (rade ade) *Noun* – **1.** a bright red mixed drink, which is extremely sweet and tasty. **2.** a cheap version of the popular Kool Aid drink. **3.** powdered red drink. **Eg.** *"Yih kin always tell when somebody bin drinkin' red ade, cuz dey whole mout be glowin' red like dey Dracula or someting'."*

Red Mole (rade mowle) *Noun* – **1.** an extremely valuable and mineral-rich form of top soil, which is red in colour, and having a tendency to stain clothes with its rich pigment. **2.** really fertile top soil. **Eg.** *"If you gah red mole in yo ya'ad, you set fa life cuz you kin grow all kinda veggatebbles ta live off a when times hard in Cayman."*

Red Shank (rade shainke) *Noun* – **1.** a small land crab, having a dark shell and reddish orange and purple claws and feet. **2.** the *'Halloween Crab'*; a species of crab from the family of *Gerarcinidae*. **3.** a burrowing crab which can be found on local beaches and around Almond and Willow trees throughout the Islands. **Eg.** *"If ah Red Shank pinch yoh foot, da docta gah needa cut im off wid ah laser."*

Reverse Back (rih-vurce bak) *Verb* – **1.** to move in a backward direction. **2.** to move in reverse. **3.** to back up. **4.** to shift into reverse gear and proceed. **Eg.** *"Ok Sonny, just reverse back ah lil' bit, n' you should be alright."*

Rich Boy (ritch boyy) *Noun* – **1.** one who appears to have come into a significant amount of cash. **2.** the child of wealthy parents. **3.** a young man who has just been paid for services rendered, or received money as a result of an allowance, a raffle, or other means. **Eg.** *"I dunno why Trenwick always play like he nah ah rich boy when he well know he daddy own half ah Cayman."*

Rich Gyal (ritch gyaall) *Noun* – **1.** a snobby young lady who tends to treat others as if they are of a lower class. **2.** a young girl born to wealthy parents. **3.** a young lady/ woman who has just been paid for services rendered, or received money as a result of an allowance, a raffle, or other means. **Eg.** *"Wendy always go on like she one rich gyal when she get pay; spennin' out all ah her money on make-up n' clothes, when she well know she gah all kinda bills ta pay, an her baby fadda nah helpin' wit nuttin'!"*

Righted (rye-did) *Adverb* – **1.** having a significant amount of understanding or sensibility to be considered sane. **2.** normal. **3.** in good mental or physical health or order. **Eg.** *"Miss Winnie always tell me I nah righted wheneva I go on like ah edieyut."*

Right Right Now (ryte ryte now) *Adverb* – **1.** immediately; to this instant. **2.** now. **3.** not yesterday, not tomorrow, not ten minutes from now. **4.** without delay. **Eg.** *"So you sayin' Marsha wah supposed ta come ova now right? She comin' right right now? or she gah one ah dem watches wit Cayman Time built in?"*

Rile Up (ryle up) *Verb* – **1.** to irritate or vex. **2.** to fill with anger. **3.** ready to fight. **4.** on the verge of rioting or fighting. **Eg.** *"Wheneva da gas prices go up, people get all rile up cuz dey know da light bill and wadda bill goin' up too n' dey cyah do nuttin' 'bout it."*

Rock Bun (rawk bun) *Noun* – **1.** a traditional dessert, made from vanilla extract, coconut milk, brown sugar, cinnamon, allspice, nutmeg, salt, butter/margarine, etc...; rolled into a curly shaped bun. **2.** a tasty bun, which has a solid surface on the outside and a soft, tender inside. the whole bun is sweet throughout. **Eg.** *"I used ta help my daddy mek some good rock bun but afta Iwan flood out uwah oven, we nah really made none since."*

Rock Hole (rawk hoal) *Noun* – **1.** the area of George Town, first named in the early 20th Century, when a large hole was dug into the ground to create a well; wood ash was mixed with the well water and left to settle over time and become lye, a natural detergent. women came from miles around to the 'rock hole' to get lye to use as laundry detergent. hence, the area became known as 'Rock Hole'. **2.** the neighborhood beginning at School House Road near Boosey Shop (Solomon's Grocery) and ending at School Road, next to Young World Fashions. **Eg.** *"Some people down in Rock Hole don't even go ta Annex ta watch football."*

Rong (rawng) *Adverb* – **1.** around. **2.** in a particular region or area neighboring a place. **3.** about; on all sides; encircling; encompassing. **4.** somewhere nearby. **Eg.** *"Try so moo from rong me wit dah fooshniss 'bout you love me but you 'accidentleh' kiss somebody else."*

Rosemary Broom (roze-may-reh brume) *Noun* – **1.** a homemade broom; made of twigs and leaves from the *Rosemary Tree*. **2.** a great broom for sweeping out wattle and daub houses. **3.** a multi-purpose broom used for sweeping the house, and also sweeping sand yards. **Eg.** *"Granny say her daddy use ta put ah wallopin' on her brudda Avis wit da rosemary broom wheneva he misbehave."*

Row (ruw) *Noun* – **1.** a noisy dispute or quarrel; commotion. **2.** noise or clamor. **3.** to quarrel noisily. **4.** to scold. **Eg.** *"If you mess up my pants wit dah marka my mama gah row wit me n' den I gah come lookin' fa you."*

Rubba (ruh-bah) *Noun* – **1.** a common pink eraser found in most school supply kits. **2.** a device, as a piece of rubber or cloth, for erasing marks made with pen, pencil, chalk, etc. **Eg.** *"Teacha always use ta tell me dat if I fuhget ta bring my rubba ta school I coulda always use hers."*

Rubba Tree (noh-teet) *Noun* – **1.** a *Rubber Tree*. **2.** any tree that yields latex from which rubber is produced, esp. *Hevea brasiliensis*, of the spurge family, native to South America (and also found in the Caribbean), the chief commercial source of rubber. **3.** a tall tree with long, sturdy limbs, and large tentacle-like vines. **Eg.** *"Georgey used ta lowe swingin' on dah rubba tree when we wah in Troot Fah Yoot School."*

Rubry (rubb-reh) *Noun* – From East End; **1.** rugby; a game played by two teams of 15 players each on a rectangular field 110 yards long with goal lines and goal posts at either end, the object is to run with an oval ball across the opponent's goal line or kick it through the upper portion of the goal posts, with forward passing and time-outs not permitted. **Eg.** *"Less go play some rubry since football season done now!"*

Rum Point (ruhm poynte) *Noun* – **1.** the peninsula at the northwesternmost part of North Side. **2.** a residential community which borders the Cayman Kai area in the District of North Side. **3.** the area where (according to legend) a boat carrying casks of liquor (thought to be rum) ran aground, giving the area its name. **4.** one of the best places to hang out, play volleyball, drink, eat, and socialize on the weekend. (also pronounced: '***Rum Pint***') **Eg.** *"I know I nah seen yah all week, but juss wait till Sundeh n' we kin go Rum Pint n' chill out."*

Run (ruhn) *Verb* – **1.** to cause an action or event to happen. **2.** to perform a particular act. **3.** to operate. **4.** to cause another person to flee or feel unwelcomed. **Eg.** *"If L.B. come rong yah again, try so gi im two dollas n' run im bug he bizniss"* or *"When I started diss taxi twenny odd years ago, I diddn' realize how much dedication it tecks ta run ah business."*

Run Down (runn down) *Noun* – **1.** a popular Caribbean dish made primarily of ground provisions, including potatoes, yams, broccoli, etc. mixed with various forms of meat (i.e. chicken; various fish) or plain vegetables and coconut milk. it tends to be altered according to the interests of the chef and the consumer. **2.** a traditional Sunday lunch. **Eg.** *"Anytime I finish ah good bowl ah run down, jess gimme ah hummuck n' I good fah da ress ah da day."*

Runnin' Ants (ruh-nin ahntz) *Noun* – **1.** small black or dark brown ants which are harmless to humans. **2.** one of the few non-biting species of ants on Grand Cayman. **3.** picnic ants; sugar ants. **4.** ants which can be found running in circles, but appear to be going nowhere. **Eg.** *"Anytime ya see sumting spill on da ground like juice or milk or someting, and ya leff it deh fa good lil' while, dah when ya gah see dem runnin' ants comin' out all ova da place."*

Runny Belly (ruh-neh beh-leh) *Noun* – **1.** frequent and watery bowel movements. **2.** diarrhea: an intestinal disorder characterized by abnormal frequency and fluidity of fecal evacuations. **Eg.** *"Hear wah I tell you, doon' eat nuttin' Felisha cook cuz it jess gah gi ya runny belly."*

Run Off (ruhn awff) *Verb* – **1.** to make a photographic reproduction of (printed or graphic material), especially by xerography. **2.** to photocopy. **Eg.** *"Sweetie, when you go ta work tomorrow, try so run off cupple ah ya fadda birt certificates fa meh."*

Russell's (ruh-sulz) *Noun* – **1.** the venue of several afterhour 'sessions' during the mid-1990s. **2.** a fun place to enjoy reggae music in the middle of the night during the 1990s. **Eg.** *"One time deh wah so much cars down by Russell's, dat Police hadda come direct traffic so people could go home."*

Saheppmihgeezumpiece (suh-hep-muh-jee-zum-pee'ce) *Interjection* – **1.** so help me. **2.** listen closely, or else. **3.** if it is the last thing I do. **4.** an expression of disbelief. **Eg.** *"Sweetie, if you doon' hurry n' go bayde so we kin go shoppin' at Fosta's, saheppmihgeezumpiece, I gah mek ya go wit ya dirty skin!"*

Salt Air (sawl't eere) *Noun* – **1.** an invisible mist of salt-laced moisture which emanates from the sea. **2.** salty air. **Eg.** *"Anytime salt air blow on Richy car, he cyars it straight home n' wash it off."*

Salt Spray (sawlt sp'ray) *Noun* – **1.** the scattered particles of salt water from the ocean. **2.** the salty mist which comes from the sea during tropical storms, cold fronts and hurricanes. **3.** one of the worst things to get on one's car. **Eg.** *"Awleh! I gah try hurry n' get home ta wash my car b'fore da salt spray mess up my engine 'n russ up my paint."*

Sand Yard (sahn ya'ard) *Noun* – **1.** the tradition of backing buckets of sand from various beaches to spread throughout one's yard. **2.** a yard full of beach sand, regardless of the proximity to the ocean. **Eg.** *"Granny say erry Christmas, widdout fail, she hadda mek sure she gah ah nice sand yard or else she couldn' sleep."*

Sanapee (sah-nah-pee) *Noun* – **1.** a common centipede. **2.** any of numerous predaceous, chiefly nocturnal arthropods constituting the class *Chilopoda*, having an elongated, flattened body composed of from 15 to 173 segments, each with a pair of legs, the first pair being modified into poison fangs. **Eg.** *"One time, ah sanapee bite my gyalfriend on her lip in da middle ah da night n' I hadda rush 'er hospital. Boy we wah scared."*

Sapappah (suh-pah-puh) *Noun* – From Old People Times/From West Bay; **1.** a really bad beating. **2.** the worst beating of one's life. **3.** a demonstration of screaming and hollering while being beaten with a seemingly indestructible Tamarind Switch. **Eg.** *"Hurry up n' lemme play da PlayStation now or else I gah tell Pahpah n' he gah gi you ah good sapappah t'night."*

Sawannah (suh-wah-nuh) *Noun* – **1.** *Savannah;* a rural community within the district of Bodden Town. **2.** the area which encompasses all parts between Spotts Newlands Road and Hirst Road, including Pedro St. James, ICCI, CountrySide Shopping Village, Savannah Meadows and Savannah Acres. **3.** the birthplace of many Cayman cowboys. **4.** Cayman's self-proclaimed countryside. **Eg.** *"I hear dem boys from Sawannah lowe horses more dun dey lowe woman."*

Shoole (s'hule) *Verb* – **1.** to water at the mouth, as in anticipation of food. **2.** to show excessive pleasure or anticipation of pleasure. **3.** to drool. *Noun* – **4.** saliva running down from one's mouth. **Eg.** *"Mama cookies so good dey mek ya shoole till ya tung fall out."*

Scranton (skrah'n-tun) *Noun* – **1.** the area encompassing all parts between Linwood Street and Tigris Street. **2.** the neighborhood directly behind Burke Maude Plaza. **3.** one of the best places to find someone who can cook beef and bake heavy cakes. **Eg.** *"Wheneva dem ladies from Scranton cook, errybody be lickin' dey fingas cuz it taste so good."*

Sea Beef (see beef) *Noun* – **1.** a hard, slug-like animal with pinkish-coloured flesh underneath a tough shell that is commonly found stuck to rocks on the ironshore. **2.** a *Slug* or *Leech-like* parasite with a striped, stoney shell which spends it's entire life stuck to a rock, ingesting minerals from the ironshore. **Eg.** *"Boy, you mussa lick yoh head, cuz I know it nah ga be me eatin' no Sea Beef tonight."*

Sea Egg (see aye'g) *Noun* – **1.** a type of *sea urchin*, usually black and covered in long prickles. **2.** one of the most painful objects to step on while walking in the sea. **3.** an ugly egg-like creature which lives in small caves beneath the ocean **Eg.** *"One time ya could jess reach in da wadda by Bob Soto's n' pick up ah hand full ah sea eggs."*

Sea Grape (see gray'p) *Noun* – **1.** *Coccoloba Uvifera*; a species of flowering plant in the *buckwheat* family (Polygonaceae), which grows primarily near the sea or large bodies of salt water. **2.** a sprawling bush or small tree that is found on beaches throughout the Cayman Islands and the Caribbean, as well as southern Florida. **Eg.** *"Red Shanks always diggin' holes unda my grape tree."*

Sea Itch (see ih'che) *Noun* – **1.** a bulbous, brownish-green floating algae (a close relative to '*Sea Weed*') which is extremely irritant to the human skin. **2.** a floating algae armed with the potency of a jellyfish, but disguised as a harmless Sea Weed. **3.** the ruination of many snorkeling trips for tourists and locals alike. **Eg.** *"Hush nah? I know you just get sting by Sea Itch, but you nah gah mek so much nize det dah whole Public Beach kin hear."*

Seb'm Mile Beach (she'b'm myle beech) *Noun* – **1.** the amazing Seven Mile Beach. **2.** a long crescent of coral-sand beach on the western shore of Grand Cayman. **3.** the most popular and most developed area of Grand Cayman. **Eg.** *"All kine ah man be tryin' check touriss woman wit dey American twang n' kin barely speak English."*

Seet (seeet) *Noun* – **1.** pssstt. **2.** to generate a hissing sound with one's mouth as a form of flattery or communication. **3.** to call one's attention by making a hissing sound with one's mouth. **Eg.** *"ssssssttttt... sweetie yah waugh ah ride home? I kin keep yah comp'neh yih'nah?"*

Serasee (sir-see) or **Cerasee** (sare-ah-see) *Noun* – **1.** *Momordica charintia*; a climbing vine of the cucumber and pumpkin family. **2.** a popular tea bush. **3.** a tea made from the boiled leaves of the *Serasee Plant*, which is said to be good for strengthening the blood, relieving jaundice and purging and promoting healthy skin. **Eg.** *"My ahn'deh always gimme some ol' stink Serasee Tea ta drink when my belly hurtin' but I cyah stand it man."*

Shades (shay-dz) *Noun* – **1.** any pair of dark sunglasses. **2.** spectacles that are darkened or polarized to protect the eyes from the glare of the sun. **3.** a mandatory fashion accessory in today's world. **Eg.** *"Billy always gah be wearin' he shades when he cruisin' chrew town in he new Benz."*

Shtrink (sh'treengk) *Verb* – **1.** 'shrink'; to contract; reduce. **2.** to cause (a fabric) to contract during finishing, thus preventing shrinkage, during laundering of the garments made from it. **3.** an act or instance of shrinking. **Eg.** *"I hate da way my clothes always come out all shtrink up afta ya wash um da first time yih'see?"*

Sick-eh (sihk-ehh) *Noun* – **1.** a pet name for a sick person. **2.** one who is always sick. **Eg.** *"Come yah, sick-eh. Lemme try so help you cuz all you gah do is cough all ova da place and mek me sick too."*

Siddown (sih-down) *Verb* – **1.** relax. **2.** to make less tense, rigid, or firm. **3.** to release oneself from inhibition, worry, tension, etc. **Eg.** *"Boy you bess try so siddown or else I gah lick ya dong fa bodderin' meh ova stupidness."*

Silva Tatch (sih'l-vah) *Noun* – **1.** *Coccothrinax proctorii*; the Silver Thatch Palm; a native thatch tree, of which the leaves were a key ingredient in the Cayman economy up until the mid-20th Century. **2.** the leaves from a tree of the same name which are used for creating thatch products, including roofs for houses, bags, rope, hats, and bowls. **3.** Cayman's only endemic palm. **Eg.** *"Wen it hot like diss, juss gimme ah good silva tatch hat, ah hummock n' some swanky, n' I kin mek it chrew, no problem."*

Simpa Wiweh (sim-puh wy-weh) *Noun* – **1.** the *Aloe Vera* plant. **2.** any aloe of the species *Aloe Vera*, the fleshy leaves of which yield a juice used as an emollient ingredient of skin lotions and for treating burns. **3.** a leaf containing a puss-like liquid which can be used to correct children from using foul language. **Eg.** *"Boy, if ah ketch ya liyin' again, I gah put 2 gallons ah Simpa Wiweh in yo mout."*

Sir Turtle (sur tur-tuhl) *Noun* – **1.** Cayman's 'Uncle Sam'. **2.** the mascot of the Cayman Islands. **3.** one of Cayman's most prominent National Symbols. **4.** a pegged legged turtle which became the national symbol for Cayman Airways, when it was purchased from Suzy Soto in 1960 for $1.00. **Eg.** *"If dey eva try ta get rid ah Sir Turtle again I know it gah be pure ruction cuz errybody lowe ah Sir Turtle".*

Skinny Lee-Lee (s'kih-neh-lee-lee) *Noun* – **1.** an abnormally thin person. **2.** seemingly anorexic. **3.** a very lean or slender; emaciated person. **4.** unusually low or reduced; meager. **Eg.** *"Mama, Telford callin' me "skinny-lee-lee" again. Tell im stop or I gah bung up all two ah he eyes."*

Slave Wall (slay'v wohl) *Noun* – **1.** an incomplete wall built by slaves as the last line of defence against pirate raids. **2.** a long wall located in Bodden Town, which rises to a height of six feet in some places and meanders for about a half mile in a horse-shoe shape through the rocky backwoods of town. **3.** a wall which was allegedly cursed by the slaves who built it, one day before slavery was abolished in Cayman. (also called: **Drummond's Wall**) **Eg.** *"I use ta tink det Slave Wall wah juss ah pile ah rocks until Uncle Jimmy explain wah happen when dey build it."*

Smit Barcadere (s'mitt bar-kuh-deer) *Noun* – **1.** *Smith Cove.* **2.** a beautiful cove located on South Church Street, featuring a relaxing array of tropical trees, warm, clear waters, and magnificent sunsets. **3.** a popular beach for locals and tourists alike. **Eg.** *"Any Caymanian who tell you dey nehwa bayde in da sea at Smit Barcadere is fulla lies."*

Smoke Pan (smoke pahn) *Noun* – From Old People Times; **1.** a one gallon paint can with a wire handle, half full of sand, with holes above the level of the sand to increase air flow. **2.** an empty paint can filled with burning dried cow dung or black mangrove wood to ward off mosquitos. **3.** a crude but inexpensive mosquito repellant. **Eg.** *"Man, if we hadda walk rong wit ah smoke pan deez days, Cayman would be so stink."*

Soldier Crab (sol-jah krahb) *Noun* – **1.** the *Hermit Crab.* **2.** a burrowing crab of the genus *Gelasimus*, of many species. the male has one claw very much enlarged, and often holds it in a position similar to that in which a musician holds a fiddle, hence the name. **Eg.** *"Anytime Miss Anny tie her hair in ah bun, it look like ah soldier crab."*

Some Lil' Way (sum lill wey) *Adverb* – **1.** in some way or another. **2.** however possible. **3.** the easiest and quickest way without going to an extreme. **4.** somehow; with the help of a miracle. **Eg.** *"I nah finish school so I hadda fine some lil' way ta meck sure my chillrin get dey ehjacayshun."*

Sore Up (soh're upp) *Adverb* – **1.** full of aches and pains due to soreness; tenderness. **2.** fatigued in the muscles. **Eg.** *"When I wah small, my granfadda used ta leave uwah bunkey all sore up when me n' my brudda wah misbehavin'!"*

Sour Tap (suw-ah tapp) *Noun* – **1.** a very painful strike or blow to one's body. **2.** a beating, by hand or with an instrument. **3.** a licking. **Eg.** *"Cuz, when Foggy gi him one sour tap yih'see? Even ta he dead granny mussa feel it."*

Space Out (s'pay'ce-owtt) *Adverb* – **1.** spaced out; daydreaming. **2.** dreamily or eerily out of touch with reality or seemingly so; spacey. **3.** absentminded dreaming while awake. **Eg.** *"I used ta be space out in class erry day cuz it wah borin' n' Ms. Lorna diddn' know how ta teach Social Studies."*

Spanish Rock (spah-nish rawk) *Noun* – **1.** an area in Bodden Town which is approximately north-west of the Guard House. **2.** an area of Bodden Town first inhabited by Christian Moors in 1632 when they were outcast from Spain. They inhabited the island for forty years until their young men were lured into the effort to recapture Jamaica for the King of Spain. Spanish Rock was deserted by 1672. **Eg.** *"When I use ta hear my daddy talkin' ta Mista Fred 'bout Spanish Rock, I taught it wah ah type ah music."*

Spoily (s'poyle-eh) *Noun* – **1.** one who is childish and spoiled. **2.** juvenile. **3.** rude and unruly. **4.** full of contempt for rules. **5.** determined to have one's way. **Eg.** *"Wathcha spoily nah? He face always gah be screw up like somebody tryin' kill im."*

Spotts Straight (spawt'z stray'te) *Noun* – **1.** a straight road, originating from the end of *Old Prospect*, and ending at the *Spotts Dock*. **2.** the venue of many fatal car accidents. **3.** one of the longest stretches of straight road on Grand Cayman. **Eg.** *"Cuz, you shoulda see how I had sink da clutch n' pop 'er in fiff gear up by Spott's Straight. It wah sweet man."*

Spray Rain (s'praye reen) *Noun* – **1.** intervals of light rainfall and windiness. **2.** drizzle. **3.** a very light rain. **Eg.** *"If you wauh get ta yoh car, ya bedda run quick, cuz it juss spray rain out deh now but it gah get worse dun dat."*

Spult (spul't) *Adverb* – From West Bay; **1.** spoiled; having the character or disposition harmed by pampering or oversolicitous attention. **2.** rude and unruly. **3.** full of contempt for rules. **4.** of the impression that one's own self-interests are predominant over all others. **Eg.** *"David always be goin' on spult cuz he cyah get he way all da time."*

Stall Out (stawl owt) *Verb* – **1.** to receive an insult so terrible, it stops one from moving. **2.** to stop moving; die; as in a vehicle. **3.** a fatal, unexpected embarassment. **Eg.** *"You shoulda see when Clarence went go acks Renee ta prom; I know he nah get ah stall out when she tell im Brinwell had already acks 'er from lass year"*

Starve Out (stah'rve owt) *Adverb* – **1.** really greedy. **2.** having a strong or great desire for food or drink. **3.** excessively or inordinately desirous of wealth, profit, etc.; avaricious. **4.** keenly desirous; eager. **Eg.** *"Boy, Tubby starve out yih'see? All he do is eat like food goin' out ah style."*

States (stay-t'z) *Noun, Pl.* – **1.** an abbreviation of the United States of America. **2.** a republic in the Northwestern Hemisphere comprising 48 conterminous states, the District of Columbia, and Alaska in North America, and Hawaii in the North Pacific. **3.** the best place to get away for shopping on a long weekend. **Eg.** *"If I eva get tiyud ah Cayman, I goin' live someway in da States."*

Stick-Up (stik upp) *Noun* – **1.** a profane use of the middle finger. **2.** to use profanity through sign language. **3.** to 'flip the bird'. **Eg.** *"Ahh-haah! Dah wah ya get fa showin' people stick-up. Ya shoulda get more dun two weeks detention."*

Stilt House (stihl't howce) *Noun* – From Old People Times; **1.** a traditional *Old Caymanian House*, built on a series of stilts (3-5ft. above ground) to avoid flooding during severe storms (i.e. Nor'westers, Hurricanes, etc...). **2.** a classic Caymanian house. **Eg.** *"When Mr. Artha turn he stilt house inta ah store, some people tell im he wah crazy."*

Stoopidness (stoo-pid-niss) *Adverb* – **1.** pure foolishness. **2.** annoyances and irritatants; trouble. **3.** really outrageous. **4.** uncalled for. **5.** making no sense whatsoever. **Eg.** *"I tink it's pure stoopidness ta go rent movies when I jess pay $1,599.00 fah ah new DSS system."*

String Up (streeng upp) *Adverb* – **1.** goofy looking. **2.** ridiculous; silly; wacky; nutty. **3.** to hold someone off of their feet or compromise their footing. **Eg.** *"Mr. Parley say dah guy had look all string up when he come in he shop lass week."* or; *"If you don't stop messin' rong wit dem bad boys you gah get string up by Police one ah deez days."*

Striker (stry-kah) *Noun* – **1.** a twenty-foot long stick, made from a *Cherry* tree, and having a hole carved out of the tip, to insert a pair of metal 'prongs' for grabbing. the striker is used when fishing for conch and/or lobster, from the comfort of a small boat in waters which are 20ft. deep or less. the fisherman generally uses a 'water glass' to find the catch, and 'strike' the animal carefully with the prongs. **2.** a long stick, similar to a fruit picker, used to collect lobster and conch from the ocean floor. **Eg.** *"One time my Unka Charley had drop he striker in da wadda n' hadda go diwe it up quicktime b'fore it wash way."*

Style (stile) *Noun* – **1.** the current trend or fashion. **2.** the thing to do. **3.** a mode of living, as with respect to expense or display. **4.** a mode of fashion, as in dress, esp. good or approved fashion; elegance; smartness. **5.** something to be followed. **Eg.** *"I don't care wah nobody say. I nah runnin' around in dem sissy slippers and bug eye glasses just ta be in style."*

Sucka Tree (suh-kah tree) *Noun* – **1.** a Banana or Plantain tree. **2.** any of several tropical and subtropical tree-like herbs of the genus *Musa* having a terminal crown of large leaves and usually bearing hanging clusters of elongated fruits. **3.** a banana sucker. **4.** a plantain sucker. **Eg.** *"Ah good way ta practice darts is ta pelt um at ah sucka tree in da back yard when nobody nah ah'rong."*

Suck Finga (suk feeng'gah) *Noun* – **1.** the digit of the hand that is favoured during finger sucking, usually the thumb. **Eg.** *"Caroline, get dah suck finga outta yoh mout right now!. You's ah big ten year-old gyal now yih'nah?"*

Sumpm'n (suhm'p'm) *Noun* – **1.** something. **2.** some thing; a certain undetermined or unspecified thing. **3.** a person, place, thing, time, or location, which has not been clearly specified. **Eg.** *"Man, sumpm'n doon' feel right about Leroy comin' ta pick me up wit my ex-husband in da car."*

Surrud (suh-rud) *Adverb* – From Old People Times (seafaring navigation) **1.** to the south. **2.** a cardinal point of the compass lying directly opposite north. **3.** lying toward or situated in the south; directed or proceeding toward the south. **Eg.** *"Dey say if ya ho use facin' ta da surrud, ya might get good prewailin' winds in da affanoon."*

Swanky (swaieng-keh) *Noun* – **1.** a special treat made from a *Civil Orange (sour orange)*, brown sugar and water which is mixed or blended into a drink similar in taste to lemonade. **Eg.** *"Man, when summa be hot, gimme ah good glass ah swanky n' ah hummuck n' I good ta go."*

Sweet Sop (sweet sop) *Noun* – **1.** *Annona squamosa;* (*Sugar-apple, Sweetsop or Custard Apple*) a species of *Annona* native to the Caribbean and the tropical Americas **2.** a semi-evergreen shrub or small tree reaching 6-8 m. tall. the fruit flesh is edible, white to light yellow, and resembles and tastes like custard. the seeds are scattered through the fruit flesh; they are blackish-brown, 12-18 mm long, and hard and shiny. **Eg.** *Durin' Hurricane Ivan, I watch one sweetsop hold on ta da tree fa dear life, n' it made it chrew... jess like me n' you."*

Sweet Up (swee-dup) *Verb* – **1.** to brown-nose. **2.** to curry favour; behave obsequiously. **3.** to play on one's emotions for personal gain. **4.** to spray cologne, lotion, or any other odorous substance on oneself. **Eg.** *"Anytime I waugh sleep ova by Cristy house, I juss go n' sweet up my daddy n' he meks me get my way"* or; *"Carden comes ta work all sweet up erry mornin' cuz he tryin' get Molly Ann ta like 'im."*

Swell Head (sweh'l hed) *Adverb* – **1.** full of ego. **2.** pertaining to or characterized by egotism. **3.** given to talking about oneself; vain; boastful; opinionated. **4.** looking after one's own self interests. **Eg.** *"Erry time Lily tell Brandon det he dress sexy, he be walkin' rong wit one swell head da size ah George Town."*

Ss

Tally Wappin' (tah-leh wah-pin) *Noun* – From Old People Times; **1.** a really bad beating. **2.** to have one's credibility destroyed as a result of losing a fight. **3.** to have one's butt kicked. *Slang* - **4.** to get kicked to pieces. **Eg.** *"I doon' know how chrew it is, but dey say Randal gi Freddy ah good tally wappin' fah steppin' on he Jordan's."*

Tamarind (tahm-rinn) *Noun* – **1.** the pod of a large, tropical tree, *Tamarindus indica*, of the legume family, containing seeds enclosed in a juicy acid pulp that is used in beverages and food. **2.** the tree from which the notorious *'Tamarind Switch'* is made. **Eg.** *"Lemme tell ya something, if somebody mek ya da real Caymanian Tamarind Jam, you gah lick yoh fingas off when you taste it."*

Tamarind Switch (tahm-rinn switch) *Noun* – **1.** a large branch, freshly picked from the *Tamarind Tree* for the specific purpose of disciplining a child. **2.** the most feared word in a child's vocabulary. **From Old People Times** – **3.** a stick and leaves from the *Tamarind Tree*, used to discipline unruly, disrespectful children. **Eg.** *"If yoh Daddy eva sen ya fah ah Tamarind Switch, ya know somebody gettin' beat n' it might even be you."*

Tatch (tah'che) *Noun* – **1.** *Thatch*; a material, as straw, rushes, leaves, or the like, used to cover roofs, grain stacks, etc. **2.** the leaves of various palms that are used for thatching. **3.** something resembling thatch on a roof, esp. thick hair covering the head. **4.** a material used for plaiting various household items, including hats, fans, brooms, and plates. **Eg.** *"My Aunt Miriam kin mek anyting outta tatch if ya tell 'er wah ya waugh."*

Tatchin' (tah-chin) *Adverb* – From Old People Times; **1.** *Thatching*; the process of weaving, twisting, tying, or by any other means, working with thatch leaves and thatch products. **2.** an early occupation for many of the poor families throughout the Islands, who would work tirelessly to create thatch products such as ropes, twine, hats, plates, brooms, etc. for sale at local and overseas markets. **3.** the process used in creating large projects, such as the traditional 'thatch roof'. **4.** an endangered Cayman tradition. **Eg.** *"Anytime ya see Granny Linette doin' some tatchin' dah mean she in ah bad mood."*

Teck (tek) *Verb (used with object)* – **1.** take; to get into one's hold or possession by voluntary action. **2.** to hold, grasp, or grip. **3.** to receive or be the recipient of. **4.** to convey in a means of transportation. **Eg.** *"Ransford say if Wilson doon' stop messin' wid im, he gah teck back dah new Playstation game he jess buy im fah he birtday."*

Tee-Dee (tee-dee) *Noun* – From West Bay; **1.** a close personal friend, usually female. **2.** reference to someone without using their real name. **Eg.** *"Aye Tee-Dee, pay attention nah? You cyah see people tryin' talk sense in yoh head?"*

Teef (teef) *Noun* – **1.** a thief. **2.** one who steals, esp. secretly or without open force; one guilty of theft or larceny. *Verb* – **4.** to take (the property of another or others) without permission or right, esp. secretly or by force. **Eg.** *"Lissin' yah man: You cyah hear I nah gah no money ta lend you cuz somebody teef my wallet lass night?"*

Teets (teetz) *Noun* – **1.** a common nickname for someone who loves to smile and grin a lot. **2.** pl. of tooth. **3.** the group of instruments designed for biting and chewing one's food. **Eg.** *"I gah ah cousin name 'Teets' but he leff Cayman when he wah small n' I nah seen im since."*

Tereckleh (tuh-reck-leh) *Adverb* – **1.** later. **2.** the not-so-distant future. **3.** a future time to come. (also pronounced: 'ereckleh', 'dereckleh', or 'areckleh' in some areas) **Eg.** *"Lemme know wah ya doin' tereckleh so I kin plan ma day bedda."*

Tenna (teh-nah) *Noun* – **1.** any person of East End origin or descent. **2.** one who lives in East End, the easternmost district on Grand Cayman. **3.** an East Ender. **Eg.** *"It might be biased since my family from East End but I know dem tennas is some ah da bess fishaman een da Caribbean!"*

The Juice (duh joo'ce) *Noun* – **1.** the latest gossip. **2.** juicy gossip; fresh news. **3.** the latest talk of the town. **Eg.** *"Aye, hurry up so gimme da juice nah? I waugh know wah happen while I wah in Hialeah."*

The '32 Storm (duh tir-deh too stawrm) *Noun* – **1.** a massive hurricane which struck the Sister Islands in November 1932, claiming the lives of 108 persons, including 29 children under age 10. **2.** the worst storm in the history of the Cayman Islands. **3.** the 'killer storm' which left many dead and others either injured or mourning on Little Cayman and Cayman Brac, where houses were ripped to shreds and trees were left completely bare. **Eg.** *"My granny say if we wah livin' when da '32 storm had hit, we woulda know wah real disasta is."*

The Republic (duh rah-pubb-lick) *Noun* – **1.** the district of West Bay. **2.** the place where West Bayers are kept. **3.** Weh Bay. **Eg.** *"Aye, watch wah ya sayin' bug West Bay rong Arnold; he from the Republic."*

Tick Dope (tik doap) *Noun* – From Old People Times; **1.** a really toxic chemical (shampoo) which was used to remove ticks and other insect from cows. **2.** a flea bath for cows. **3.** a tick repellent. **Eg.** *"If dey had keep usin' tick dope on dem cows, we woulda nehwa had no beef on diss Island. Dem farmas use ta use too much n' it kill off all da cows."*

Ting (ting) *Noun* – **1.** *thing*; a material object without life or consciousness; an inanimate object. **2.** some entity, object, or creature that is not or cannot be specifically designated or precisely described. **3.** a fact, circumstance, or state of affairs. **Eg.** *"Man! Moo da ol' slimy ting offa me!"*

Tired Out (ty-urd owt) *Adverb* – **1.** extremely exhausted to the point of dehydration and delirium. **2.** enervated, tired, exhausted, fatigued **2.** weary of struggling against misfortunes. **Eg.** *"I be so tired out afta I finish playin' football det I cyah barely liff my hand ta feed my face."*

Tiyud (tye-udd) *Adjective* – **1.** lacking the ability to move forward with energy or enthusiasm. **2.** sluggish. **3.** weak and futile. **4.** unable to compete against stronger forces, due to one's lack of assertiveness, drive, and will. **5.** undesirable. **6.** worn out. **Eg.** *"Dean say he hadda get rid ah dah ol' tiyud Lexus he had cuz it wah always on da bum."*

Tobacca (ta-bah-kuh) *Noun* – **1.** tobacco; any of several plants belonging to the genus *Nicotiana*, of the nightshade family, esp. one of those species, as *N. tabacum*, whose leaves are prepared for smoking or chewing or as snuff. **2.** the habit of smoking tobacco. **3.** tobacco products, including: cigarettes, chewing tobacco and cigars. **Eg.** *"Chewin' tobacca is one real nasty habit dat my Granfadda couldn' give up no madda how hard he try."*

Toe Peak/Toe Punch (toh peek/toh puntch) *Noun* – **1.** a really powerful kick in the game of football where the player uses only his/her toes to launch the ball to the other side of the field. **2.** the wrong kick to use for close range targets. **Eg.** *"Anytime Boggy chrow ah toe peak and miss da ball, aftawurds he be blamin' da grass 'bout it too long or somebody spill wadda on it."*

Tom Fool Day (tawm-fool dey) *Noun* – **1.** April 1st of each year. **2.** the day of which one may become the victim of a practical joke or trick; also known as *'April Fools' Day'*. **3.** a day of pranks and gags, which, while fun at times, can also lead to public deception, lies and unjustified trickery. **Eg.** *"Erry Tom Fool Day, Renton always come wit da same ol' tricks n' be gettin' on people nerves."*

Tong (tawng) *Noun* – **1.** town. **2.** a contraction of 'George Town'. **3.** the capital district of Grand Cayman. **Eg.** *"Aye, tanks fah gi'in me ah liff ta Tong yih'hear? My car nah workin' n' I nah had no money ta ketch no bus."*

Tourisses (toh-rih-siz) *Noun, Pl.* – **1.** one or more persons who have travelled to the Cayman Islands for pleasure and exlploration. **2.** a group of tourists. **3.** visitors to the Islands who may arrive either by plane or by cruiseship. **4.** very friendly visitors who are always welcome to the Cayman Islands. **Eg.** *"Lass week I see one whole pile ah tourisses walkin' dong North Church Street. I taught I wah in da middle a Pirate's Week or someting."*

Towna (taow-nuh) *Noun* – **1.** a *'George Towner'*; one whose origins and upbringing lie in George Town, the Capital district of Grand Cayman. **2.** any person from the district of George Town, which includes (but is not limited to); Scranton, Bell Bell, Swamp, Central, Harlem, Windsor Park, Palm Dale, Tropical Gardens, Spotts, Dog City, Bodden Road, Templeton and Monkey Town. **Eg.** *"It gah always be competition between districts, so I don't see no harm in respeckin' ah towna fa representin' my district."*

Tree (tree) *Noun* – **1.** 'three'; a cardinal number, 2 plus 1. **2.** a symbol for this number, as 3 or III. **3.** being one more than two. **Eg.** *"I doon' know way Tommy get all ah diss money from but I hear he gah 'bout tree cars in he yard park off ketchin' duss."*

Turtle Head (tur-tull hed) *Noun* – **1.** having an abnormally long neck and a knobbly head, resembling that of a turtle. **2.** one whose head resembles a turtle. **3.** a long-necked person. **Eg.** *"Sometimes it good ta play wit udda people, but Randy went too far when he call Minwell ah turtle head in front ah he gyalfriend."*

Turtling (tur-tull-eeng) *Noun* – **1.** turtle fishing; to hunt for turtles, especially as an occupation. **2.** one of the most prominent occupations responsible for the growth and development of the Cayman Islands during the early to mid 20th Century. **Eg.** *"Gran-fadda always used ta lowe tellin' stories 'bout how he used ta go turtling, spear fishnin' and pongin' conch on da iron shore."*

Twiss Foot (twiss foot) *Adverb* – **1.** lacking the ability to kick a football in a straight line. **2.** badly coordinated feet. **3.** having a really wobbly step while walking. **4.** an injured foot. **Eg.** *"We coulda win da five-a-side game, but ol' twiss foot Bingum hadda go kick da ball ova da goal post."*

Twissin' Strand (twih-sin strahn) *Verb* – From Old People Times; **1.** the traditional art of twisting and weaving thatch leaves into a rope. **2.** a technique which was used to create thatch rope for various uses. Twisted strand ropes were also used to barter for goods at various stores throughout the islands. **Eg.** *"My mama say Granny n' her five sistas used ta be twissin' strand erry Friday night, so dey could do some weekend shoppin' on Satdehs."*

Um (uh'm) *Pronoun* – **1.** them. **2.** those. **Eg.** *"Aye, bring dem sweet padaydas ova yah so ah kin peel um nah?"*

Unna (uh-nah) *Pronoun* – **1.** you people. **2.** you all. **3.** the lot of you. **4.** a reference to two or more persons as a collective. (see also: *unneh* – used by select districts) **Eg.** *"If unna don't stop teasin' me I gah tell my daddy."*

Unneet (uh'n-eet) *Noun* – **1.** underneath. **2.** below the surface or level of; directly or vertically beneath; at or on the bottom of. **3.** at a lower level or position; on the underside. **Eg.** *"Sweetie, go so look unneet da seddee n' see if yih kin find dah blasted t.v. remote."*

Unneh (uh'n-eet) *Pronoun* – **1.** you people. **2.** you all. **3.** the lot of you. **4.** reference to two or more persons as a collective. (see also: *unna*) **Eg.** *"I hear unneh nah get ta go Miami again cuz Michael cuss out yo daddy."*

Up'na-bush (uh'p'nuh bush) *Noun* – **1.** into the bushes. **2.** into a grassy area, overgrown pasture, or thicket. **3.** advancement into an area overgrown by weeds and grass and having many tall trees and wildlife. **Eg.** *"My Pahpa use ta cyar me up'na-bush ta look mangos erry Satdeh."*

Urr (erh) *Pronoun* – **1.** our. **2.** the nominative plural pronoun. **3.** a form of possessive case of *'we'* used as an attributive adjective. **Eg.** *"Diss is urr country, nobody cyah tell us wah ta do unless we mek um get 'way wid it."*

Uwah (uh'wah) *Pronoun* – **1.** our (a form of the possessive case of *'we'* used as an attributive adjective). **2.** belonging to us. **Eg.** *"Less have ah party so we kin have fun wit uwah friends nah?"*

Veggatebbles (vedge-ah-teb-ulz) *Noun, Pl.* – **1.** *Vegetables.* **2.** plants which are cultivated for an edible part such as the root of the beet, the leaf of spinach, or the flower buds of broccoli or cauliflower. **3.** ill-tasting foods which are healthy, but not as tasty as fruits. **Eg.** *"I heare Hurley's always gah da bess selection ah veggatebbles."*

Video Max (vid-ee-oh mackz) *Noun* – **1.** one of the first tapeclubs on Grand Cayman to feature pre-recorded *Beta* and *VHS* tapes. **2.** a popular tapeclub during the 1980s. **3.** a tape rental facility (formerly) located in The Village Shopping Centre. **Eg.** *"One time I had rent one movie from Video Max, kepp it fa 17 munts, n' dey nah even know I had it. Da funny ting is I wah still rentin' udda tapes same time."*

Voylent (voye-lent) *Adjective* – **1.** a mis-pronunciation of the word 'violent'. **2.** acting with or characterized by uncontrolled, strong, rough force. **3.** having or showing great emotional force. **Eg.** *"I keep tellin' Sherry det if she don't stop messin' wit my curlin' iron, one ah deez dayz I gah get voylent."*

Vwicks-Sahwe (vwikz-sahwhe) *Noun* – **1.** the ointment known as '*Vicks Salve*'. **2.** an old wives remedy for any ailment. **3.** a special ointment used for treating the common cold, aches and pain. **Eg.** *"Even if ya head doon' hurt too bad, still try so rub some vwicks sahwe on it and it might feel bedda."*

Vwe (v'w-ee) *Noun* – From West Bay; **1.** the letter 'v' - pronounced with a strong Caymanian accent. **2.** the 22nd letter in the common alphabet. **3.** the letter before 'w' and after 'u'. **Eg.** *"P, Q, R, S, T, U, Vwe."*

Vv

Wah (wuh) *Adjective* – **1.** what. **2.** used interrogatively as a request for specific information, or to inquire about the character, occupation, etc., of a person. **3.** used interrogatively to request a repetition of words or information not fully understood, usually used in elliptical constructions. **4.** was. **Eg.** *"I dunno wah you doin', but I nah stayin' yah tonight."*

Wah'henameis (wuh-hee-neem-iz) *Pronoun* – **1.** an unclear reference to a male person who cannot be named. **2.** that guy. **3.** the man. **4.** him. **Eg.** *"Uncle Albert, wah'henameis out deh lookin' fah you again."*

Wah'hernameis (wuh-hur-neem-iz) *Pronoun* – **1.** an unclear reference to a female person who cannot be named. **2.** she. **3.** her; that woman. **4.** your friend. **Eg.** *"When I go back ta work tomorrow, wah'hernameis bedda nah be sittin' by my desk again or else it gah be me n' her."*

Wah'itnameis (wuh-itt-neem-iz) *Pronoun* – **1.** a nonspecific reference to someone or some thing, without giving any useful description whatsoever. **2.** that thing. **3.** the object; the place; that guy. **4.** someone or something which cannot be described in any way. **5.** the object or person which cannot be named. **Eg.** *"Mummy, way da wah'itnameis? I waugh show Silvia wah I got fah Christmas."*

Wahoo (wah-hoo) *Noun* – **1.** *Acanthocybium solandri*; an elongated, dark blue scombrid fish found in tropical and subtropical seas. **2.** a popular fish among deep sea fishermen. **3.** a fish, having flesh that is delicate and white and regarded as very good in quality. **Eg.** *"Some people say Wahoo is da Cayman dolphin, n' some say dey diffrunt. I doon' care cuz dey goin' in my belly same way."*

Wyahcallit (wy-ah-kawl-it) *Adverb* – **1.** that thing. **2.** whatever it is. **3.** the object. **4.** the thing that cannot be described at this time. **Eg.** *"Purnell, go tell Randy muss bring da wyahcallit from out my tool shed please?"*

Wayahsayin? (wy-yih-say-in) *Adverb* – **1.** what's up. **2.** how are you today. **3.** an informal greeting to someone familiar, but yet unknown. **4.** a form of acknowledgement between males. **Eg.** *"Wayasayin' man? I neva know dah wah you det had dah new Civic wit dem bad ol' rims."*

Wadda Knee (waugh-dah nee) *Noun* – **1.** water on the knee; a general term used to describe excess fluid that accumulates in or around the knee joint. **2.** knee effusion. **3.** a traumatic injury to the knee which is most dreaded by athletes, especially football players. **Eg.** *"Bobo, anytime ya go kick ah football, mek sure ya doon' miss, cuz yih gah dihwellup wadda knee n' ya doon' waugh dah."*

Wash Out (waush owt) *Noun* – **1.** an old wives solution to any form of illness that is not immediately apparent. **2.** to purge one's digestive system via a laxative. **3.** of, pertaining to, or constituting a laxative; purgative. **4.** to administer a laxative of some sort, whether it be natural, over-the-counter, or clinical. **Eg.** *"Mel say anytime she feel bad, her mama would tell 'er she need ah good wash out."*

Water Glass (waugh-dah glah'ce) *Noun* – **1.** a makeshift wooden box (around the size of a milk crate) which is is partially submersed into the water to magnify the contents of the ocean floor, allowing fisherman to select an area to drop anchor, and also to pick lobsters and conch effortlessly, with a 'striker' (see *Striker*). **2.** a glass-bottom box used for fishing. **Eg.** *"Ol' Pah say whenevea he had he water glass wid im' he used ta bring back all kinda fish n' lobstas n' conch n' ting."*

Wattle n' Daub (wot-ul-n-dawb) *Noun* – From Old People Times; **1.** a system of building materials used in constructing houses. **2.** a woven latticework of wooden stakes called *wattles* is *daubed* with a mixture of clay and sand and sometimes animal dung and straw to create a structure; it is normally whitewashed to increase its resistance to rain. **Eg.** *"National Trust juss pay good money ta preserve one wattle n' daub house dong by Purny grasspiece"*

Ww

Waughhh! (waugh) *Interjection* – **1.** an expression of excitement and amazement. **2.** a word used to express one's enthusiasm or interest in what he or she is seeing or hearing. **3.** a verbal salute. **Eg.** *"Waughhh!! I neva know you had get yoh new Civic! It look Sweet doh."*

We (wee) *Noun* – **1.** the letter 'v' - pronounced with a Caymanian accent. **2.** the letter before 'w' and after 'u'. **Eg.** *"P, Q, R, S, T, U, We..."*

Wear Out (wear owt) *Adverb* – **1.** the state of being wasted or diminished gradually by rubbing, scraping, washing, etc. **2.** fatigued; exhausted. **3.** to make or become unfit or useless through hard or extended use. **4.** to dress in new clothes for a special occasion at a special place. **Eg.** *"Cindy had borry my new miniskirt ta wear out ta one reggae concert n' get drink spill on it."*

Weebles (wee-bullz) *Noun, Pl.* – **1.** a series of small brown worms, often found in fiber-rich products such as flour, grain, corn meal, corn flakes and oats. **2.** a very pesky disappointment to have in one's breakfast cereal. **3.** little worms that love corn meal. **Eg.** *"Mummy look yah, my Lucky Charms fulla weebles again."*

Wee-Wee (wee-wee) *Verb* – **1.** to expel waste fluids from one's body through urination. **2.** to eliminate urine. **3.** to take a leak. **4.** to 'pee'. **Eg.** *"Thelma always gah wee-wee at da worst possible time, especially when we watchin' ah good movie."*

Weh Bay (weh bay) *Noun* – **1.** the District of *'West Bay'*. **2.** one of the most densely populated districts on Grand Cayman. **3.** the place where *"West Bayers'* live. **4.** a great place to find a sea captain, a fisherman, or a seafood chef. **Eg.** *"Fifi say Weh Bay too far ta be drivin' ta work, but wah 'bout dem people det gah ketch bus from all ah way East End?"*

West Bay (wess bay) *Noun* – **1.** one of Grand Cayman's five voting districts. **2.** the northernmost area of Grand Cayman. **3.** where *'West Bayers'* were born. **4.** a great place to find a thatchmaker, a prominent politician, or a Justice of the Peace. (also called: **Weh Bay**) **Eg.** *"Dah time when Prince Edward had come West Bay ta open Barkers Park, I diddn' get ah autograph cuz he security wah too tight."*

Wex (wexx) *Adverb* – **1.** vexed to the point of nuclear status. **2.** extremely irritated; annoyed; provoked. **3.** in need of a pillow to scream in, so as to avoid a criminal record. **4.** red in the face with anger and malice. **Eg.** *"Anytime ya see my daddy come outside in he short pants n' no shirt, dah mean he 'wex' an' somebody gettin' beat."*

White Holes (wyte holez) *Noun, Pl.* – **1.** large patches of skin or close-shaven hair, following a really bad haircut. **2.** the result of a bad haircut done at home by a relative or close friend. **3.** a terrible hair cut which usually results in the person having to bald their entire head to save face. **Eg.** *"Waaaahhhh! Look ah all ah dem white holes, man! Yoh barba wah drunk when he cut yoh hair ah wah?"*

Whitey-Whitey (wye-deh wye-deh) *Adjective* – **1.** having white marks or dye on one's clothing, usually from old paint or white marl. **2.** dry skin (usually elbows and knees) which appears lighter than the rest of the body. **Eg.** *"Mummy ya gah any lotion? I waugh wear my new shorts but my knees look all whitey-whitey."*

Wholesome Bakery (hole-sum bay-k'reh) *Noun* – **1.** a landmark cafeteria and bakery which was located on the waterfront of George Town and famous for its freshly baked breads, patties, pastries, milkshakes and other treats. **Eg.** *"I almost cried tears when dey closed down Wholesome Bakery yih'nah. I used ta kill off some serious milkshakes and patties up in dah place yih'see?"*

Wihkayshun (wih-kay-shunn) *Noun* – **1.** vacation; to go on holiday. **2.** a period of suspension of work, study, or other activity, usually taken for rest, recreation, or travel; recess or holiday. **3.** leisure time away from work devoted to rest or pleasure. **Eg.** *"I hate dah way Troy always be goin' on wikayshun y'see? All he do is brag 'bout way he bin."*

Winwud (win-wudd) *Noun* – **1.** windward. **2.** toward the wind; toward the point from which the wind blows. **3.** pertaining to, situated in, or moving toward the quarter from which the wind blows. **4.** of or on the side exposed to the wind or to prevailing winds. **Eg.** *"Bobo, try so see way da stink fish scent comin' from? I tink it comin' from da winwud, but I nah sure, since it nah no wind blowin' now."*

Wit (witt) *Preposition* – **1.** Caymanian pronunciation of the word 'with'. **2.** accompanied by; accompanying. **3.** in correspondence, comparison, or proportion to. **Eg.** *"Doon' mess wit me or else I gah tell my daddy."*

Womit (waugh-mit) *Verb* – **1.** to vomit. **2.** to throw up. **3.** to eject the contents of the stomach through the mouth; regurgitate; throw up. *Noun* – **1.** the matter ejected in vomiting. **Eg.** *"Juss da smell ah fish cookin' meks me feel like I gah womit."*

Wompa (wawm-puh) *Noun* – From Old People Times; **1.** a sandal made from old automobile tires lashed with palm fibers between the toes and around the heel. **2.** a very comfortable traditional Caymanian shoe. **3.** the name teenagers give to any shoe that is not current or trendy. **Eg.** *"If I had ah dolla fa errytime my Granny talk 'bout how she miss her wompas, I would be ah zillionairre."*

Wored Out (wore'd owt) *Adverb* – **1.** dog tired; utterly exhausted; worn out **2.** dehydrated; drained of energy or effectiveness; extremely tired; completely exhausted. **Eg.** *"I diddn' beliewe it b'fore but now I undastand wah granny mean when she use ta talk 'bout how she wah wored out from all da runnin' up n' down."*

Wum (wum) *Pronoun* – **1.** them. **2.** the objective case of 'they', used as a direct or indirect object. **3.** people in general. **Eg.** *"Uh-angh! I tell you you could have one or two chips, but I diddn' tink you woulda tek all ah wum!"*

Wush (wuh'sh) *Noun* – **1.** extremely untidy, unkempt hair. **2.** having a very bushy head. **3.** a very embarrassing state of one's hair. **Eg.** *"I always gah be tellin' Alric ta comb he wush or else termites gah start livin' up in deh."*

Wutless (wutt-liss) *Adjective* – **1.** worthless. **2.** without worth; of no use, importance, or value; good-for-nothing. **3.** low; despicable. **4.** lacking in usefulness or value. **Eg.** *"My neighbah call her husband ah wutless man, cuz he loss he job n' den went out drinkin' wit he severance pay."*

Ww

Xtra

Xtra (eks-trah) *Adverb* – **1.** excessive in nature. **2.** too much. **3.** to carry oneself in a flamboyant way. **4.** to behave extravagantly. **4.** eccentric and misunderstood. **Eg.** *"I cyah stand da way Darcy go on when she get rong Mandy n' da crowd ah dem – dey jess too xtra man."*

Some people go on 'xtra' during Pirates Week as part of the festivities.

Yaad (yah'd) *Noun* – **1.** the place of one's residence. **2.** the ground that immediately adjoins or surrounds a house, public building or other structure. **3.** the residence of one's parents. **Eg.** *"When ya finish watchin' tee-wee jess come pick me up by my yaad. I nah gye'n no way."*

Yaah'ndah (y'aah'ndah) *Adverb* – **1.** yonder. **2.** being in that place or over there; being that or those over there. **3.** being the more distant or farther. **4.** at, in, or to that place specified or more or less distant; over there. **Eg.** *"Mama I goin' up yaah'ndah ta see if Cootsy waugh come ova fa dinna awright?"*

Yabba (yah-buh) *Noun* – **1.** one's mouth. **2.** the source of conversation. **3.** a talkative mouth. **Eg.** *"Wah? Gyal try hush yoh yabba, talkin' bout you see my friend drinkin' beers down by Mr. Early grasspiece."*

Yah (y'ah) *Adverb* – **1.** here. **2.** to or toward this place; hither. **3.** in or to this very spot. **Eg.** *"Aaanhh, huuhhhh... Come yah! Way you tink you goin? Ya lil' brute."*

Yalla Tail (yah-lah tayle) *Noun* – **1.** slang for *Yellow Tail*; a specific reference to the Yellow Tail Snapper. **2.** any of several other fish with a yellow caudal fin. **3.** *Ocyurus chrysurus;* a small West Indian snapper. **Eg.** *"Next time I go fishnin' I cyar'in my big line cuz lass time one big ol' yalla tail had bite off dah ol' flimsy one I had deh."*

Yeow! (y'owh) *Slang* – **1.** what's up? **2.** hello my friend. **3.** how's it going? **4.** oh my gosh! is that really you? **Eg.** *"Yeow wah goin' on? Errying aw'rite ah wah? I nah see you since we graduate John Gray."*

Yy

Yih'nah (yih-nuh) *Slang* – **1.** you know. **2.** can you believe it? **3.** a conversational filler, equivalent to "um" and occasionally repeated over and over. **Eg.** *"Gee, she diddn' eable gimme time ta mek up my mind yih'nah; She juss run up'na bahtchroom ta wash her hair so she kin go look man."*

Yoh (y'oh) *Pronoun* – **1.** your. **2.** a form of the possessive case of YOU used as an attributive adjective. **3.** one's own. (used to indicate that which belongs to oneself or to any person). **Eg.** *"Cuz, dah yoh football rong da back deh?"*

Yonda Hill (yawn-dah hihl) *Adverb* – **1.** a hill not far from here. **2.** a nearby hill. **3.** the closest hill. **Eg.** *"I lowe it when I kin ride up yonda hill cuz it be fun goin' down on da udda side."*

You Boy (yoo boy) *Pronoun* – **1.** you there. **2.** an interjection directed at a particular male person, without using a given name. **3.** hey you. **4.** reference to an unknown individual. **Eg.** *"Aye you boy, you cyah see my dog nah gah mess wit you if you don't mess wit him? Why you hadda go kick afta im fah? He shoulda eat ya alive"*

You Gyal (yoo g'yull) *Pronoun* – **1.** you there. **2.** an interjection directed at a particular female person, whose name is currently unknown. **3.** an indirect reference to one's female friend; from the 2nd person. **Eg.** *"Pssssttt, you gyal. You cyah pass meh some choong gum ah wah?"* or; *"You gyal look yah one minute. I waugh acks ya sump'm 'bout uwah mahts homework."*

Youngy (yung-eh) *Noun* – **1.** a common nickname for an immature mango. **2.** the youngest one. **3.** one which has not reached its maturity. **Eg.** *"I teachin' my nephew 'bout all da types ah mangoes, includin' turney, youngy, scruffy, etc. so he kin know wah dey name when he grow up."*

Yy

Zee • Zekiel

Zee (zee) *Noun* – **1.** the 26th letter of the alphabet, a consonant. **2.** a written or printed representation of the letter *Z* or *z*. **3.** any spoken sound represented by the letter '*Z*'. (also pronounced: **zed**). **Eg.** *"I doon' care wah you say, the word is 'zee' not 'zed'. Yoh teacha mussa nah learn ya nuttin' in school."*

Zed (zed) *Noun* – **1.** the last letter in the alphabet. **2.** another way of pronouncing the alphabet known as '*zee*'. **3.** the 26th letter of the English alphabet, a consonant. (also pronounced: **zee**) **Eg.** *"Dey say some people say 'potayto' n' udda people say potah-to. Well den nobody bedda na say nuttin' ta me fa sayin' 'zed' when I talkin' 'bout ah 'zee'."*

Zekiel (zee-ki-yell) *Noun* – **1.** one half of the comedic duo known as '*Sookie and Zekiel*'. **2.** a prominent Caymanian comedian and cultural enthusiast. **Eg.** *"I used ta lowe goin' Harquail jess ta watch some good Sookie and Zekiel skits. Dey wah da hardest boy."*

The letter 'Z' spelled with Poincianna seed pods.

Acknowledgements

Special Thanks from the Author

"I would like to thank everyone who contributed to this project in any way as your input is not only invaluable to Caymanology but to the Cayman Islands as a whole.

First, I would like to thank my wife, Leticia Goring for her encouragement and support, my parents Ted & Inez Goring, brother Kurt Goring, sisters Tania Ebanks (nee Goring) and Sarah V. Goring and brother-in-law Avons Ebanks for word contributions, fact checking, marketing advice, editing and proofreading.

Many thanks to all Testimonial Contributors and Supporters (too many to name) and my nine year-old son, Nolan Goring, for being the inspiration and purpose for this publication (you are the future). May God bless you all."

-- Kevin M. Goring

Credits

The Cayman Islands National Archive - (research and definitions for words in its reference library directory)
  - especially; *Bush Med'sin; Cayman-made Boats; Crabbin'*
  - some info has been paraphrased throughout this publication and may not be recognised immediately.

Gov.ky - (general info about the Cayman Islands)

Eso.ky - (statistical information)

Photo Credits

All photos provided by the author, Kevin M. Goring, except those found on various public domain websites or purchased by the author for promotional use.

Printed in the USA
CPSIA information can be obtained
at www.ICGtesting.com
LVHW011207240724
786358LV00001B/108